*In order
to enrich understanding
and enhance the reputation of
theatre scholarship as a vital activity, the
American Society for Theatre Research has created
this Special Issues series as a vehicle
for the explication of
theatre history.*

# EDWARD GORDON CRAIG

## AND *THE PRETENDERS*

### A PRODUCTION REVISITED

BY FREDERICK J. MARKER

AND LISE-LONE MARKER

Published for the
American Society for Theatre Research
by
Southern Illinois University Press
Carbondale and Edwardsville

**Library of Congress Cataloging in Publication Data**

Marker, Frederick J
Edward Gordon Craig and The pretenders.

(Special issues—American Society for
Theatre Research)
Bibliography: p.
Includes index.
1. Ibsen, Henrik, 1828-1906. Kongs-emnerne.
2. Ibsen, Henrik, 1828-1906—Stage history—Denmark—Copenhagen. 3. Craig, Edward Gordon, 1872-
1966. I. Marker, Lise-Lone, joint
author. II. Title. III. Series: American Society
for Theatre Research. Special issues—American Society for Theatre Research.
PT8872.M3    792.9'2    80-27481
ISBN 0-8093-0966-1

Printed in the United States of America
Designed by Richard Hendel

CONTENTS

# LIST OF ILLUSTRATIONS

# ACKNOWLEDGMENTS

During the course of the research for and preparation of this study, the authors have enjoyed the fullest cooperation of the following institutions, to which it is a pleasure to be able to extend our thanks publicly: the Danish Royal Theatre in Copenhagen, Universitetsbiblioteket in Copenhagen, the Danish Theatre Museum, the Guthrie Theater in Minneapolis, the Fischer Rare Book Library of the University of Toronto, and, by no means least, the Bibliothèque Nationale in Paris. In particular, we are grateful to Niels Peder Jørgensen and Marianne Hallar of the Royal Theatre Library and to Mlle. Cécile Giteau, Conservateur en chef des Collections théâtrales a la Bibliothèque de l'Arsenal, and her able assistant Mme. Coron for their generous help and courtesy. The warm hospitality and expert advice extended by Professor André Veinstein, Université de Paris, made our work in the Collection Craig both infinitely easier and more pleasant. A debt of gratitude of a very tangible nature is due to the Humanities and Social Sciences Committee of the University of Toronto for travel grants in support of this research. We are also deeply grateful to the Publications Committee of the American Society for Theatre Research for its sponsorship of this book, and to Stephen W. Smith of Southern Illinois University Press for his helpful editorial guidance. On the personal side, it would be remiss indeed to overlook the force of the inspiration derived from the recollections of those who actually witnessed this famous production and have remembered it. Our affection and gratitude go to the indomitable Thorvald Larsen, whose long career in the theatre has

been a genuine source of inspiration to those around him, and to Henry Christensen, who sat beside the glamorous Asta Nielsen on that fateful night and has never, never forgotten.

FREDERICK J. MARKER
LISE-LONE MARKER

EDWARD GORDON CRAIG

AND *THE PRETENDERS*

For that is what the
title of artist means:
one who perceives more
than his fellows, and one who
records more than
he has seen.

CRAIG, *On the Art of the Theatre* (1911)

Why do I tell you all this?—
because some day the History
of the Theatre has to be written,
and you must keep what I
write to you, and tell your descendants
to "report me and my cause aright
to the unsatisfied."

GORDON CRAIG to Johannes Poulsen (1931)

# CHAPTER ONE

## CRAIG'S LAST PRODUCTION

The plays of Ibsen seem to have exerted a profound and abiding influence on Edward Gordon Craig. As early as 1900, Craig had created an eerie, silhouettelike design project for *Peer Gynt*. For his first full-fledged professional production in London, presented under the auspices of his mother, Ellen Terry, at the Imperial Theatre in April, 1903, he selected Ibsen's early saga drama, *The Vikings of Helgeland*. Although this venture proved to be a financial failure, Craig's visionary designs for the production—in particular his now-so-familiar renderings of the luminous and towering banqueting-hall in act 2 and of the evocative, spherical death space created for the somber events of the last act—have continued to hold a permanent place in the history of modern stage design. ("Craig's scenery is amazing," Yeats reported in a letter to Lady Gregory after seeing the play—though he added, characteristically, that it "rather distracts one's thoughts from the words.")[1]

When Craig came to design *Rosmersholm* for Eleonora Duse three years later, he was more than ever determined to "leave period and accuracy of detail to the museums and to curiosity shops." "Ibsen can be so acted and staged," he argues in a program note for this production, which was presented at the Teatro della Pergola in Florence in December, 1906, "as to be made insignificant and mean. Therefore we must ever remember our artistry and forget our propensity towards photography, we must for this new poet re-form a New Theatre."[2] Craig's shadowy, impressionistic interior for the play ("a

I

vision of loveliness," thought Duse) seeks to reveal that "profound impression of unseen forces closing in upon the place" which he felt to be the essence of Ibsen's drama: "we hear continually the long drawn out note of the horn of death." Craig's provocative conception for *Rosmersholm* met a ready response among Italian critics and artists who saw the performance.

Il palcoscenico appariva trasformato, veramente trasfigurato, altissimo, con un'architecttura nuova, senza più quinte, di un solo colore fra il verde e il cilestrino, semplice, misterioso e affascimante, degno insomma di accogliere la vita profonda di Rosmer e di Rebecca West.[3]

[The set—very high, newly designed, without side scenes, of a single color between green and light blue—appeared transformed; (it was) simple, mysterious, fascinating, worthy, in short, of embracing the inner life of Rosmer and of Rebecca West.]

As we know, however, and as so often happened in Craig's career, an acrimonious dispute ended all hopes of continuing this potentially fruitful collaboration with Duse. Hence his design project for *The Lady from the Sea*, Duse's favorite Ibsen vehicle, was never realized—though the highly abstract architectonic setting which he drew for this play reminds us once again of his determination to eliminate the distraction of pictorial scenery by creating instead "a place which harmonizes with the thoughts of the poet."[4]

All these earlier approaches to Ibsen may, however, in a sense be regarded as a prelude to the crucial and controversial production of *The Pretenders* which, just twenty years after Craig's brief association with Duse, marked his last direct involvement in the practical theatre. As one of the astonishingly small handful of actual productions in which Craig ever took part during his long career, his *Pretenders*, which opened at the Danish Royal Theatre in Copenhagen on November 14, 1926, must be said to command a central place in any analysis of his artistic physiognomy. Viewed from a somewhat different angle, this production must also be accorded its due importance in any stage history of Ibsen's plays during the postnaturalistic period. Nevertheless, the relative inaccessibility of primary source documents in this case seems to have led most scholars to discuss this particular Craig project only briefly (if at all) and then almost invariably in the light of the persuasively positive comments by Craig contained in *The Mask* and in his opulent portfolio of published

designs, entitled *A Production, Being Thirty-two Collotype Plates of Designs prepared or realized for "The Pretenders" of Henrik Ibsen and produced at the Royal Theatre, Copenhagen, 1926* (1930).[5] In fact, however, a very substantial body of unpublished source documents—most of them also untranslated—does exist and must be taken into account if a more balanced view of this final Craig production and its relationship to his theories is to be achieved.[6]

Ferruccio Marotti has usefully called attention to some of the thorny methodological problems which flourish in the field of Craig studies. The truth about any given performance must very often be sought in documents other than the *public* statements of Craig and his contemporaries; even when (as with his *Pretenders*) extensive design material exists, the process of translation from design to stage is much more complicated than we might imagine; and (especially in the case of *The Pretenders*, one might add) we must avoid "making any false connection between the projected theatrical work and the public reception of that work."[7] More recently, a comprehensive bibliographical survey of Craig archives reemphasizes "the need for outside evidence as corroboration and corrective" and urges us "to look beyond Craig archives for material with which to establish a true picture."[8] Thus, although *A Production* affords invaluable insight into the poetics and working methods of the artist, it remains at best a partial and at times a very misleading guide to the actual theatrical event. (That it is, of course, an integral artistic phenomenon in its own right is a point which its author stresses. "If the artist is a dreamer of the very practical kind, he does not worry very much as to whether the dream will be realized or no—because it *is* realized. A dream once dreamed properly is a reality inasmuch as it is worked out from beginning to end. It sounds queer to you, this . . . but no . . . surely you have dreamed dreams?"[9] For the theatre historian, however, it is essential to analyze the interplay of a variety of other, more objective sources and documents that can help us to view Craig's designs and published commentary in a clearer perspective.

Paramount among these sources are the actual production records preserved in the archives of the Danish Royal Theatre—a rich mine of primary evidence which, as we shall come to see, includes promptbooks, "signal books" containing light and sound cues, the stage manager's records and floor plans, and the official daily journal of rehearsals and performances. Each of these documents contributes its share of information, not only about the 1926 *Pretenders* but also, for

purposes of comparison, about the two earlier productions of this play staged at the Royal Theatre. Copious newspaper reviews of the Craig performance supplement these preproduction records, and these reviews (subject to Marotti's admonition!) serve to clarify the controversy surrounding the production and its actual impact upon an audience. Unfortunately, the Royal Theatre's customary procedure of taking working photographs of the settings had in this instance to be abandoned for lack of time. Nevertheless, a small number of publicity stills and caricatures did appear in the daily press—notably in the newspaper *Politiken*, which printed three scene photos and several witty caricatures with its review—and these afford at least some visual impression of the costuming and the style of acting, if not of Craig's scenery. [10] Although none of Craig's own set designs for *The Pretenders* is to be found among the Royal Theatre's archives, a set of designs and preliminary sketches for the costumes in this production is preserved there and presents an unusual little puzzle of its own.

While it would be a grave error indeed to overlook the Danish production sources on which this study proposes to draw, it could be almost equally misleading to treat these sources in isolation from the complementary documents that are to be found among the Craig papers housed in the Bibliothèque Nationale in Paris. If the Royal Theatre archives provide the only reliable guide to the production as it ultimately appeared on the stage, it is from Craig's personal notebooks, preliminary plans and sketches, draft letters, and private memoranda in the Collection Craig that one must seek to derive a more complete impression of the artist himself, of his ambivalent attitude toward the *Pretenders* project, and, above all, of the nature of his involvement in the actual production process. His own "book" for the play—an interleaved copy of the 1918 translation by Farquharson Sharp that is filled with interpretational jottings, early designs, later rehearsal comments, notes on light, sound, and movement cues, and a great deal else—is an extremely revealing record quite different in kind from either *A Production* or from the Danish promptbook preserved in the Royal Theatre Library. Another illuminating source of information is the exchange of letters between Gordon Craig and Johannes Poulsen, the Danish actor-director who first conceived the idea of inviting Craig to Copenhagen to assist him in staging a jubilee performance of Ibsen's drama. This brief correspondence tells a touching story of a friendship—but it also provides valuable clues to the nature of the working relationship between Poulsen and Craig and

the extent of their respective contributions to this enterprising undertaking.[11]

The practical situations in which Edward Gordon Craig found an opportunity to test his theories in practice were extremely few in number, and scholars have come to recognize that a fuller and more complete knowledge of each of them is essential to a balanced understanding of his contribution to the modern theatre. It is with this consideration in mind that the Craig-Poulsen interpretation of *The Pretenders* is here "revisited" in circumstantial detail. With the possible exception of the Moscow *Hamlet* in 1912—which has been the object of so much useful critical investigation in recent years—perhaps no other Craig production affords such scope for a detailed analytical study of the process and the problems involved in translating Craig's inspiration and his projects into tangible theatrical reality.

CHAPTER TWO

STAGE HISTORY

Although clearly not among Ibsen's most popular plays on the stage, *The Pretenders*, the first of his dramas to gain a permanent place in the repertory of the Scandinavian theatre, boasts a vigorous and fascinating production history. It is against this solid background of tradition that Craig's approach to the challenge of what he, rather querulously, terms "that dreadfully difficult play for intellectuals" is perhaps best understood. This expansive, five-act historical chronicle, the last of Ibsen's plays to draw upon the colorful pageantry of Norwegian history for its subject matter, dramatizes the irresistible power of a great calling and the paralyzing effects of self-doubt. Haakon, the unswerving believer in his own heroic destiny and in his ability to effectuate his great kingly thought, contends with the vacillating and reflective Skule for Norway's throne, while the violent strife between them is deliberately fostered by the diabolical Bishop Nikolas, the power-hungry impotent whose avowed purpose in life is to set in motion a *perpetuum mobile* of discord and distrust in the world.

The play was directed for the first time by the author himself at Christiania Theatre, where it opened on January 17, 1864, and held the stage for eight performances during that winter. P. F. Wergmann, whom Roderick Rudler has called the first national scene painter in Norway, was called on to design new scenery for this production, and even the services of a local antiquarian were enlisted in order to provide the proper thirteenth-century Norwegian flavor. The task of the play's first designer was thus not only to articulate the dramatic

6

1. Design by P. F. Wergmann for the
last scene of *The Pretenders*, Christiana Theatre,
1864. (Royal Theatre Library)

and atmospheric values of Ibsen's multiple, boldly contrasted stage
pictures, but also to endow them with an historical "appropriateness"
and "authenticity." Wergmann's scene design for the moonlit convent
yard at Elgesæter (ill. 1), where the defeated Skule and his son seek
refuge from the angry townspeople of Nidaros in the final scene of the
drama, seems in perfect harmony with the carefully visualized directions of Ibsen's text—itself directly inspired by the playwright's
reading of ancient Norwegian history.[1] This impressive design
(although it did not in fact win the full approval of the Christiania
production's reviewers) offers a vivid illustration of the general style
of robust pictorial solidity that was to remain intrinsic to the play's
pre-Craigian stage tradition.

The first production of *The Pretenders* at the Danish Royal Theatre,
capably directed by Johanne Luise Heiberg and first performed on
January 11, 1871, brought the play and its author to the attention of a
much broader and more cosmopolitan public—and the dramatist
promptly acknowledged suitable gratitude in that remarkable poetic
tribute, entitled "Rhymed Letter to Fru Heiberg," which he addressed to the great Danish actress.[2] To accommodate the play's ten

7

separate changes of scene, atmospheric medieval settings, designed for this production by Valdemar Gyllich, were deftly combined with a number of existing Nordic and "gothic" decors borrowed from the older repertory (notably, interiors from Boye's *Svend Grathe*, Schiller's *Maria Stuart*, Sille Beyer's Icelandic drama *Ingolf and Valgerd*, and Bournonville's splendid ballet *Valdemar*).

The scene changes themselves, particularly the more difficult ones occurring within a single act of the play, were felt by Fru Heiberg to disrupt the flow of the action, thereby dissipating dramatic tension. "In every true work of art each act is a unit, carefully measured by the author, and it is never to his advantage when this unity is broken in the middle," she argues in her autobiography. She was determined to avoid the "unjustifiable expedient which has found acceptance in all foreign theatres" of lowering a front curtain to conceal such changes, for then "the suspense of the action is relaxed, leaving the spectator completely confused about which scene concludes the act and which does not." On the other hand, she was equally unwilling to shatter the illusion by permitting the audience to "watch walls, trees, and other paraphernalia of the décor glide down helter-skelter from the sky." Instead, she devised her own system, subsequently adopted as standard practice at the Royal Theatre, of blackouts for each scene change. "When darkness is introduced . . . the audience's attention is fixed upon what will next appear to them when the darkness is again dispelled, and the illusion is maintained," she writes, adding shrewdly that "a setting never makes a greater impact than at the moment when darkness is replaced by light."[3]

Certainly the most striking feature of this production, however, was the performance of the young Emil Poulsen, soon to become one of the foremost Ibsen actors of his generation, in the role of the toothless manipulator and schemer Bishop Nikolas. "It seemed," writes Edvard Brandes in his vivid analysis of Poulsen's almost legendary interpretation of this role, "as though all the force of genius and the demonical power that Bishop Nikolas possesses were concentrated in his fierce, frightening glance." His wild eyes "searched the facial expression of every speaker as though they sought to peer into his very soul." Every intonation of his labored speech (marked by "a constant rising and falling which created the impression that the Bishop spoke only with the utmost effort"), every movement of his vivid countenance and stooped, shrunken figure was a remorseless reminder of the hatred which Poulsen conceived to be the ruling force in Nikolas's character. "Thus, a perpetual smile—sometimes bitter

8

and caustic, sometimes scornful, sometimes brilliant with demonic joy—played about his mouth." This cynical disdain suffused the Bishop's face "every time the other characters mentioned anything which, for them, belonged to what is noble and sacred."[4]

When the time at last came for the actor's son, Johannes Poulsen, to re-create the same role in the 1926 production of the play, one is left with little doubt that his performance—even in the midst of Craig's abstract shapes and non-representational blocks—continued to bear the stamp of the strongly emotional realism (the "distinctly naturalistic bent," Brandes called it) of his father's approach. It is worth noting that, as an old man, Emil Poulsen evidently acted Bishop Nikolas's death scene for his two sons, Adam and Johannes; the latter, his widow recalls, "had never forgotten it, and it had long remained his wish to act this part."[5]

Within a very few years, productions of *The Pretenders*, first at the Munich Hoftheater in 1875 and then by the Meininger troupe in Berlin the following year, served to carry Ibsen's reputation beyond the borders of Scandinavia. Especially the latter production, which ran for nine consecutive performances at the close of the third Meininger season in Berlin in June, 1876, holds particular interest—not least, of course, because of the conceivable effect which exposure to the crowd discipline and pictorial coordination of the Meininger method may have had on Ibsen himself, who pronounced their production "brilliant and spectacular."[6] Historical accuracy and ethnographic detail were again felt to be matters of utmost importance in staging the play, and Duke Georg himself journeyed "to Ibsen's northern land" to make firsthand sketches for his company's scenery and costumes. "The foreign quality shown in this production aroused such wide interest," comments Max Grube, that it helped, at least in some measure, to counterbalance the reservations of the German critics who objected to the play's "verbosity" and to the division of its focus between two heroes, Haakon and Skule.[7]

During the final quarter of the nineteenth century, the stage history of *The Pretenders* developed rapidly. In his second season as head of Christiania Theatre (1880–81), Hans Schrøder staged a splendid revival of the work, which has never been absent for long from the repertory of the Norwegian theatre. No fewer than three different productions of the play were seen in Stockholm during this period, perhaps the most interesting of which from a visual point of view was Fritz Ahlgrensson's staging of the Swedish premiere, performed at Nya teatern on January 19, 1879. For this occasion Ahlgrensson, a

gifted designer who worked at various times both in Copenhagen and in Stockholm, decided to create a group of exterior settings in which the heavier, darker tones of the older romantic style of scene-painting were eliminated and replaced by a lighter, cooler atmosphere directly influenced by the *plein air* school of contemporary landscape painting.[8] Curiously enough, the very promising revival of *The Pretenders* at the same theatre seven years later, staged this time by the pioneering Ibsen director Ludvig Josephson and starring August Lindberg, one of the most accomplished naturalistic actor-directors of the period, as Bishop Nikolas, proved a disappointment precisely *because* of Lindberg's overly restrained "naturalistic" approach to the deep-dyed scoundrelism of Ibsen's Bishop. His characterization seemed to contemporaries "well conceived and nicely developed, but so subdued and pale in coloring that the theatrical effect was lost."[9] By contrast, Emil Hillberg, the world's first Brand, drew a far more emotional and more effective Nikolas—a bold character portrait "developed with the greatest intensity and richness of nuance"[10]—when the play was taken up again at Vasa teatern in 1898 to commemorate Ibsen's seventieth birthday.

As the century drew to a close, *The Pretenders* opened once again at the Royal Theatre in Copenhagen, this time under the direction of Julius Lehmann, on October 15, 1899. Lehmann's ambitious historical revival, which was the final contribution to an Ibsen "year" that had also included new productions of *The League of Youth* and *The Lady from the Sea*, is documented by a very full range of written records and iconographic evidence that provide, as we shall see, for some direct and revealing comparisons with the later production by Craig. Five years later in Berlin, Max Reinhardt's performance of the play—the first of his Ibsen productions, staged at his Neues Theater on October 7, 1904—marked yet another important turning point in its lively stage history. Following close on the heels of major revivals at the Vienna Burgtheater in 1891 (where Bishop Nikolas was played by the keenly analytical Austrian actor Josef Lewinsky) and at the Schiller Theater in Berlin ten years later, Reinhardt's approach to such a play was distinctly different—as far from the academic realism of the Meininger as it was from the subdued naturalism of Otto Brahm. At the heart of his symbolically expressive *mise en scène* was his own deliberately unhistrionic, intellectually controlled portrayal of Nikolas as a virtual archetype of malice, "a more pleasant species of Mephistopheles, always desirous of evil."[11]

As even this necessarily abbreviated survey must indicate, then, the earlier stage history of *The Pretenders* was an eventful one, characterized by the notable regularity with which many of the best European actors, directors, and designers of the period seem to have been attracted by the challenge of what has later been called "Ibsen's first real and incontrovertible masterpiece."[12] Seen in this context, the decision by Johannes and Adam Poulsen to settle on this particular play as a perfect vehicle in which to celebrate the twenty-fifth anniversary of their acting debuts is also easily understood. In England and North America, on the other hand, *The Pretenders*— perhaps because of the "foreignness" of its subject matter—was much slower to reach the stage. Its first American production, mounted with resolute enthusiasm by an all-male cast of the Yale University Dramatic Association in April, 1907, need perhaps not detain us unduly. (Astonishingly enough, it was not until June 1, 1978, that the first professional American production of this play was attempted, under the direction of Alvin Epstein, at the Guthrie Theater in Minneapolis.)[13]

In England, Henry Irving never could be persuaded to undertake a production of the work, despite the fact that many saw in him an ideal Bishop Nikolas. Hence, London audiences were obliged to wait until February 13, 1913, before *The Pretenders*, featuring Laurence Irving in a creditable performance as the self-doubter Skule, was at long last seen at the Haymarket Theatre. The heavily pictorial, historically "authentic" quality of the Haymarket production, for which Joseph Harker and S. H. Sime were jointly responsible, seemed to some, in 1913, a belated echo of days gone by. A review in *The Spectator* characterizes the staging as "thoroughly in the grand style of realism and archaeological exactitude. We are informed that Mr. S. H. Sime, who designed the clothes and scenery, has made a special study of thirteenth-century Scandinavia. The layman is forced to admit that he is unable to distinguish the result from Wagnerian opera."[14] The style of Joseph Harker, the leading realistic scene painter at the turn of the century and during the Edwardian era, is unmistakably evident in "the vivid realisation of the old unhappy far-off world of mediaeval Norway" which is described so well in an anonymous review in *The Daily Telegraph*.

The pictorial element is, of course, powerful. Scene after scene lingers in the memory. The rude church and the fir trees, and the glimpse of fjord and rock

which we first saw, gave in a moment place and time and atmosphere. . . . The last scene of all, the court-yard of the convent from which Skule goes out to meet his doom, had a rarer and nobler grace. The gallery of arches aglow, and in the midst shadows, and all around an austere simplicity through which faint touches of clear colour came, made a deep harmony with the grandeur of the action. We do not recall decoration which interpreted and illustrated more perfectly the spirit of a play.[15]

This vivid description captures the Harker method perfectly—while at the same time it inevitably recalls to mind P. F. Wergmann's designs for the very first production of the play, mounted half a century before. In essence, little seems to have changed. Harker—one of Craig's bêtes noires and the object of thinly veiled ridicule in *A Production*—distrusted constructed settings, and pinned his faith on two-dimensional painted backgrounds which could be easily and noiselessly shifted. "The problems of stage perspective arise from the fact that the artist has a real foreground (the stage) to contend with in addition to what the back-cloth or other parts of the scene may show," he declares in 1924 in his book *Studio and Stage*. "One's difficulty is therefore blending the actual and the artificial in such a way as to make a satisfactory and convincing whole."[16]

Craig, of course, would have protested vociferously that such a "blending" can never hope to achieve either a satisfactory *or* a convincing result, because the three-dimensional presence of the living actor demands a simplified, architectonically conceived, three-dimensional stage space within which to create movement. "If a stage picture consisted of a single 'back-cloth', then you could pass all the elaborate details on to the back-cloth," he writes in *A Production*. "But then your actors would simply be acting in *front* of a *picture* and not *in the midst of a scene*" (p. 8, Craig's emphasis). He never modified his insistence that "the stage is a place to act in, not a picture to act against" (p. 14).

A related and no less unyielding principle in Craig's theatrical poetics is embodied in his adamant rejection of the overelaborated historical illusionism fundamental to Harker's approach to a play like *The Pretenders*. From the outset of his career, in his production of Purcell's *Dido and Aeneas* in 1900, Craig resolutely set out to banish all sense of historical or geographical reconstruction, to in fact be "entirely incorrect in all matters of detail."[17] This same conviction animates his spirited defense of his scenography for *The Pretenders*: "I have never been concerned," he insists in *A Production*, "in any

attempt to show the spectators an exact view of some historical period of architecture. I always feel that the great plays have an order of architecture of their own, an architecture which is more or less theatrical, unreal as the play" (p. 16). The kind of fully detailed stage directions which characterize Ibsen's text were, of course, never regarded with much tolerance by Craig: "If you meddle with the tools of a trade," he declares flatly in his gloss on the famous "rat-trap" design for the opening scene of Shaw's *Caesar and Cleopatra*, "it is best to master them—and for a dramatic writer to add stage directions to his written play, and to omit to show how these directions are to be carried out, is to tinker. In the Greek and Elizabethan drama, you will find no stage directions."[18]

"In *The Pretenders* we shall use Henrik Ibsen's dialogue and his characters but not his descriptions of the scenery," he told a Danish interviewer several weeks before the long-awaited premiere. "Local color is not something we will place very much emphasis upon—but then neither does Ibsen. We shall not try to represent the *church* or the *council chamber*, rather we shall represent the *spirit of the church, the spirit of the council chamber and the banquet*. Obviously, not all dramas take place in a historical place or in a particular historical period. In *The Pretenders*, as in *Hamlet*, a ghost appears—tell me to which historical period one can ascribe ghosts? No, drama is a product of our inner life, and we create on the stage a world for that inner life."[19]

In the light of such Craigian pronouncements as these, it is probably self-evident to add that his nonrepresentational approach to *The Pretenders* demonstrated an uncompromising repudiation not merely of the old-fashioned pictorialism of a Harker, but also of the play's entire performance tradition in general. No wonder, then, that Craig seems so eager to convince his readers that no such prior tradition had ever really existed. In *A Production* he advances the curious fiction that "when [Johannes Poulsen] came to read *The Pretenders* and its stage history, I think he discovered that very little had ever been done with the play. In fact, I believe he discovered that it had thwarted all who had ever attempted to produce it" (p. 9).

In an earlier "interview" about the production in *The Mask*, written up by Craig in Copenhagen and signed with the name "Conrad Tower" (one of the many pseudonyms used by his faithful editorial assistant, Dorothy Neville Lees), he exhibits somewhat greater regard for Emil Poulsen's immensely successful performance in the Fru Heiberg production: "This is the second time it has been presented,

the first production being in 1871, January 11th, with Emil Poulsen (father of Adam and Johannes) as Bishop Nikolas. It is a remarkable fact that the Royal Theatre was this year prepared *to revise the entire production* and present the play without being tied to its older method of presentation."[20] No mention is made of Julius Lehmann's intervening revival of the play at the Royal Theatre in 1899, however—though a full list of the costumes and properties for this production (annotated in English for the visitor's benefit) is to be found among Craig's papers in the Bibliothèque Nationale!

It would be a mistake to assume, meanwhile, that the storm of critical controversy which broke over Craig's production was somehow prompted by his defiance of established, reactionary traditions. The revolutionary ideals of the new modernism had already been firmly implanted in the Scandinavian theatre by such developments as the early visits of Max Reinhardt's company, the pioneering productions of Per Lindberg and Knut Ström at the Lorensberg Theatre in Gothenburg at the beginning of the twenties, and Johannes Poulsen's own transplantation of the Reinhardt style to the Danish Royal Theatre during the same period. Viggo Cavling, reviewing *The Pretenders* in *Politiken* (November 15, 1926), summarizes succinctly the chief cause of critical dissatisfaction with the production.

We have nothing against the simplification and stylization which Mr. Craig advocates, and we agree with him completely that the old-fashioned theatre art is often offensively glossy. But if one wants to stylize, one cannot stylize in general, but only within the framework and tone and milieu in which the play takes place—as Max Reinhardt and Jessner have done time and time again, with sublime results. And the Craigian method could undoubtedly have been applied with success here, if only the coldness of the North, the harshness of the Middle Ages, the darkness of Catholicism had been allowed to come through. Instead, we were given scenery composed of parti-colored blocks, Italian banners, French ribbon backdrops,[21] Japanese lanterns, oriental gates, and so on.

Critic after critic reiterated Cavling's basic objection: although Craig's diaphanous stage pictures might seem "like a multi-colored cloud," the impression they conveyed "had nothing to do with that bit of the Norwegian Middle Ages to which Henrik Ibsen has sought to transport us."[22] It seemed to more than one reviewer that Craig's scenery and costumes

reminded one of the staging for *The Countess Cathleen*. *The Pretenders* was served up as though it were an Irish saga, and not a ponderous Nordic drama of destiny partaking of all the violence of the Middle Ages, its proud spirit torn to pieces in the conflict between the wildness of heathendom and the Christian sense of guilt. No, Gordon Craig, regardless of how sophisticated he may be, is unable with his aestheticized designs to express that Nordic tone which pervades the play. To see *Peer Gynt* in Paris is bad, but to see Gordon Craig in Copenhagen is—in a Nordic drama—even worse.[23]

Even Svend Borberg, ardent champion of the new modernism and one of the Craig experiment's most enthusiastic partisans, was obliged to concur that "this is surely not *Ibsen!* . . . This is an Irish tale, yes exactly Irish—undoubtedly Craig has Irish blood in his veins, as do all Englishmen with imagination, and this reminds us, both in its ecstatic style and especially in its color harmonies, of the miniatures of the Irish monks, of Yeats's *Countess Cathleen*, of red hair, green peasants' coats—wonderful, but why use it for Ibsen!"[24]

The only concerted effort to vindicate the appropriateness of Craig's abstract scenography to the play at hand appeared in a lengthy feature article (the only newspaper account of the production that Craig himself bothered to save!) nearly a month after the opening. Ibsen's play, this critic insisted, is *not* realistic or even particularly "Norwegian" or "medieval" in character, but is rather "a poem of the spirit": "a dream, a symphony, a psychological drama about power— power which one may possess in the midst of his impotence, and which is at once both a joy and a curse (Nikolas); power which one may dream about and never possess, even when one holds it in his hand (Skule); and power which is peace and harmony (Haakon)."

Seen in these terms, this writer continued, Craig's conceptual staging represented the perfect visual articulation of the play's the-matic content. Groupings, stylized lighting effects, and semiabstract shapes stood out against the totally empty, nonperspective back-ground. "No mountains beyond, no forests or rustic huts, simply *the world:* the naked horizon. . . . We never believe for a moment that we are experiencing reality. We are participating in a fairy-tale, a saga, a dream, out of which the poetry grows. If anyone remembers the Russian production of *Hamlet*, which was also the work of Gordon Craig, then this is exactly the same approach, with the same poetic effect."[25]

Unfortunately, few critics shared this enthusiasm. "The Royal

Theatre ought to invite Mr. Craig to stage a Shakespearen production," Viggo Cavling's review in *Politiken* went on to observe: "Here, there would be no prefixed limitations on his imaginative impulse toward experimentation. In the Nordic drama he seems too much a foreigner." In other words, the point being urged is that—contrary to Craig's own convictions—Ibsen's historical plays do conjure up a tangible world that is not adequately served by the same abstract, dematerialized style of production that Shakespeare's plays (or even less concretely localized Ibsen dramas like *Brand* or *Peer Gynt*) might seem to admit or even to invite. Obviously the demand, in 1926, was not for a return to an outmoded *trompe-l'oeil* illusionism. Craig's right in general to seek his inspiration in the tone and spirit of the play itself, rather than in the poet's stage directions, was not in any way being challenged by the Copenhagen critics—merely his failure to conceive a theatrical image which effectively projected the concretely Nordic and medieval tone and spirit of the *specific* play before him.

The charge is a fundamental one. It has wider implications for Craig's art as a whole, and it invites closer and detailed scrutiny in the light of the actual production records and other items of evidence that survive regarding the staging of *The Pretenders*.

# CHAPTER THREE

# CRAIG COMES TO COPENHAGEN

The letters exchanged between Gordon Craig and Johannes Poulsen, a number of which have not previously been published, yield interesting insights into the vicissitudes and difficulties that beset their collaborative venture almost from the start. Poulsen, probably the most prominent exponent of the flamboyant Reinhardt style of *mise en scène* in Scandinavia during the 1920s, knew Craig's theories well and had alluded to them in an interview in the London *Daily Telegraph* (December 24, 1924), where he expressed surprise that they had apparently had so little tangible effect on the English theatre. In an impulsive note to the Danish actor-director, dated January 4, 1925, Craig conveyed his gratitude for this unexpected "expression of sympathy and friendship." The following summer, Poulsen traveled to Finland to meet with Jean Sibelius about his score for the forthcoming Royal Theatre production of *The Tempest*. Here, deeply impressed by the majestic Finnish wilderness, he conceived the idea of reviving the most powerful of Ibsen's saga dramas, in which both he and his brother Adam could appear for their jubilee and for which Gordon Craig's help could also be enlisted.

Another full year passed, however, before Poulsen was finally able to secure the theatre's official consent and then find time to write to Craig about his intention of staging *The Pretenders*. His engagingly discursive letter, dated August 12, 1926, is preserved in the Collection Craig and is reprinted (in somewhat edited form) in *A Production*. Coming as a total surprise to Craig, it invited him, in somewhat

ambiguous English, to "draw the decorations [sets] and costumes for this performance. I myself am going to set the play up, but if you would come over here and set it up with me as interpreter, we shall be very pleased indeed. You will have a free hand in every respect." Poulsen's letter goes on to describe the Royal Theatre's venerable traditions and modern technical facilities (including one of the most advanced lighting systems in Europe) and it draws attention—no doubt with an eye to the fact that the scheduled opening was less than three months away—to its extensive stock of scenery, "a gigantic decoration material and a two hundred years old supply of genuine costumes." "Not that Johannes was content to take any old Castle of Elsinore or any old grave of Ophelia and use them over and over again," Craig hastens to assure his readers, with some alarm, in *A Production*, "but he could adapt these things pretty well, and make them seem new" (p. 9).

Craig cabled his answer from Genoa ("Thank you dear friend. Will certainly do what is possible. Writing"), and followed with a letter, dated August 29, 1926, in which he affirms his eagerness to "be one of the many to celebrate the 25th anniversary of the two famous brothers Adam and Johannes Poulsen": "I will not disguise from you that my mind likes to concern itself very little with historical tragedy. It is Opera I think of most—But I will willingly design you some *Scenes* and *Costumes* and *help* you set up the play—you can produce it far better than I can—but I can *pretend* to be helping—what?" In an uncharacteristically diffident postscript, he reiterates that he "won't come if you expect *me* to produce the play for its quite beyond my forces—and besides that's your innings—I will come if on my arrival you are not going to be disappointed as to the little I can do."[1]

Poulsen's reply, dated September 14, 1926, and not previously available in print, is crucially important for the insight it provides into his own concrete (and quite un-Craigian) ideas about style and tradition.

If you do not want to get up the play, nor to make all the decorations, we should nevertheless be very pleased if you would draw 1st and 2nd act for us, *i.e.*, the scene where Inga from Varteig carries the glowing irons down through the old black stave-kirk, then the large hall, in which King Håkon feasts and the little adjoining room, from which the three women witness the men's court scene, and last not least the room in which Bishop Nikolas' great death scene takes place in the 3rd act. Norway at the time of Håkon was immensely influenced by England; thus the cathedral in Trondheim was

18

erected with the cathedral in Canterbury as a model. Later on Håkon himself built the big Håkon's Hall, which still stands in Bergen, and which is absolutely English in its whole style of building. I therefore find that both the hall and the bishop's death room very well might be English Gothic rooms from about 1240.[2]

At this point in the letter, Craig has scribbled the following marginal note: "This is strange from a disciple—one would wish him to make certain that a place if a scene for a theatre has way in way out & certain signs what it is but no date, no local habitation." Doubtless even more puzzling to Craig were the solidly pictorial views which Poulsen held of the two settings which seem to have preoccupied him most—the churchyard in Bergen where the play opens and the Bishop's chamber in the episcopal palace. In his initial letter to Craig, Poulsen had expressed his opinion that "the very first decoration has to be in the porch of or outside of one of the old pitchblack Norwegian *stavekirks*—they were made entirely of wood and resemble most of all, I find, one of the old Japanese temples in Nikko or old Siberian churches with dragon heads and bodies and swung roofs. The one in the play still stands outside Bergen in an old white fir grove—and I think that one ought to see in the deep-black church room Inga from Varteig carry the glowing hot ploughshares down the church floor." In his next letter (September 14), the Danish director is even more explicit about this particular scene.

I should think that the stave-kirk might be a great stayed [?] silhouette, covered on the sides by heavy white firs, and perhaps a rude bell-tower with grand entrance portal greatly exaggerated in perspective. The silhouette must be so big that it covers the hall that stands behind it. By doing this the interior of the hall is first used as a dark big church room with a few candles, and afterwards, when the disc [turntable stage] has been turned round, it is seen from the other side as a properly illuminated festival hall.

The letter goes on to describe a no less "authentic" view of Nikolas's chamber.

The bishop's death room I have also imagined in Gothic. I should think a back-wall similar to that of the S. Marco monastery at Florence in which Fra Angelico de Fiesole has painted Christ with all the holy men in a row underneath—of course only with an art of painting from about 1240 [means 1440?].

But all this, of course, is only propositions and ideas. If you have imagined

something quite different, then do that by all means—you must not feel yourself bound in any way.

After proposing possible costume designs and asking for Craig's terms, Poulsen's long letter concludes: "If you do not think that your time allows you to make so many decorations, then at least *the stave-kirk* and *the room in which the bishop dies.*" Ultimately, as we know, Craig's designs for these two scenes (see ills. 4, 5, 16, 17, and 18) turned out to be his best-known settings for *The Pretenders*—albeit in a form far different from anything his Danish collaborator had envisioned.

The parsimonious Royal Theatre management was greatly mollified when Craig's only conditions turned out to be payment of his fare and his hotel accommodation in Copenhagen. "I should not have to ask even this if I were not the poorest of all European theatre artists," he remarks in a registered letter dated September 17, 1926. The original of this letter seems to have been lost (or is at least omitted from the collection published by Ulla Poulsen Skou), but a much-revised draft of it is to be found in the Collection Craig. The deletions tell us perhaps more about its author's state of mind than what remains of the text. After announcing his arrival "about October 6th" and declaring his intention of bringing "many sketches & a model perhaps," Craig crosses over the following passage: "I have the 2nd act ready—the banquet scene—I think I may even send that to you in a few days—but I am anxious that the painters should make no mistakes so perhaps should be safer to bring these and explain. [Added in a marginal note:] Would not do to send the design."

After instructing Poulsen to "arrange for the other designs for scenes to be made to match with mine as well as can be," Craig again deletes a passage which could, had it reached his collaborator in clarified form, have avoided all the confusion which ultimately ensued. "But by October 6 I think (perhaps I can) shall have some useful ideas so as to be able to do all the scenes" [sentence incomplete]. "*It cant be very difficult,*" the letter concludes with a Craigian flourish. "A good month is 30 days and that should be enough (time) to remake the world. The scenes are after all nothing—what counts is the acting."

One is inevitably brought to wonder why—especially when money was not a motive—Craig should have responded to this particular invitation so readily, when so many previous and presumably more "glamorous" proposals—to stage a ballet at the Paris Opéra (for

Jacques Rouché), Shakespeare in London (for Sybil Thorndike), and opera at La Scala in Milan—had ultimately failed to entice him. Perhaps, as Denis Bablet has suggested, he was taken by the ingenuous tone of Poulsen's letters; certainly it could not have been the play itself that attracted him, for he admits to Poulsen that he had only just begun to read it. Much more likely, however, the appeal of a reputable but distinctly out-of-the-way state theatre, well removed, if only by virtue of the language barrier, from the mainstream of European theatrical activity and hence insulated from the glare of unfavorable international publicity in the event of a fiasco, must have seemed especially strong to Craig at this juncture in his career.

Whatever his motives, Craig, to judge from his replies, seemed prepared to offer some assistance but not to accept full responsibility for designing the production. Acting on this assumption, Johannes Poulsen took the reasonable step of assigning the task of designing the scenery to Thorolf Pedersen, resident designer at the Royal Theatre since 1895, when he had been given the duty of creating settings for the productions of the celebrated naturalistic director William Bloch. Although no tangible records of his proposed scenery for *The Pretenders* survive, one can easily enough envision its basic style. Remembering that even by the time that the Julius Lehmann revival of the play had opened in 1899, Pedersen was already well established in his naturalistic method, there is no reason to doubt that "the old scene-painter," as Craig liked to call him, would have looked back to the pictorialism and realistic solidity of this earlier production for his inspiration. In addition, the realistic Norwegian landscapes, mountain panoramas, snow-clad forests, and other pictorial effects which he had created for a much-admired *Peer Gynt*, starring Johannes Poulsen, in 1913 would doubtless have provided another tried-and-true model on which to pattern his latest Ibsen assignment.

In fact, as we have already begun to see, Poulsen's own ideas on the subject appear initially to have followed a not very dissimilar path. One of the most detailed of the pencil sketches found in Poulsen's promptbook[3] represents a decidedly naturalistic rendering of the palace room "in which the royal child sleeps" in act 3, scene 2 (see ill. 2), ostensibly copied from a painting by the fifteenth-century Dutch master, Hans Memling.[4] (An unused design by Craig that attempted to incorporate Poulsen's concept bears the frustrated notation: "Some 3 hours work, all to prove that all is lost in *translating* a painting by M—— on to a stage.") Along comparable lines, Poulsen's enthusiastic

2. Promptbook sketch by Johannes Poulsen
for act 3, scene 2, "Margrete on the step of
the bed platform, the cradle before her,
playing the harp." (Royal Theatre Library)

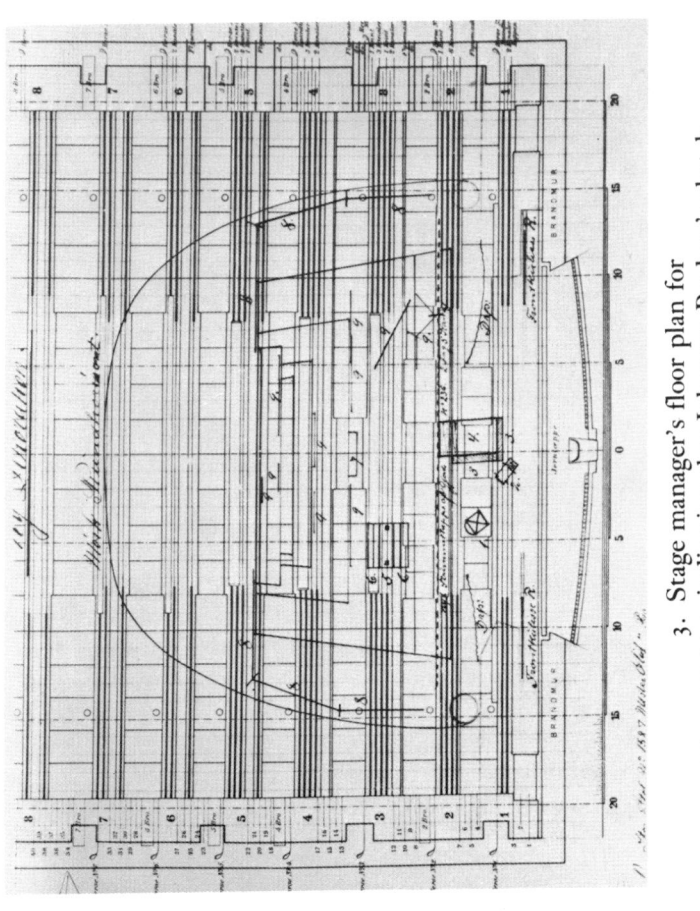

3. Stage manager's floor plan for
act 3, scene 2, indicating that Johannes Poulsen's sketch
was not used in practice.
(Royal Theatre Library)

descriptions of the authentic Norwegian "stave-kirk" with which he hoped to open the play display the same taste for historical exactitude and illusionism. Also in this case, Poulsen provided Craig with a painstakingly detailed and rather hideous pencil sketch of the edifice he envisioned, and Craig's papers in the Bibliothèque Nationale include several abandoned projects and designs that testify to his futile efforts to accommodate Poulsen's incongruously naturalistic proposal. Although it is very clear that neither of Poulsen's concepts for these scenes was ever put into actual practice (see ill. 3), they do indicate a good deal about the style which Thorolf Pedersen's art epitomized, and which would inevitably prove impossible to reconcile with Craig's ideas.

Within Pedersen's design concept for *The Pretenders*, which depended on a succession of individual built-up sets deployed on a turntable stage, it was hoped at first that Craig's presumably few contributions might subsequently be incorporated. As work in this direction progressed, nothing further was heard from Genoa. The customary *dekorationsprøver*—preliminary "scenery rehearsals" intended to establish floor plans before the actual rehearsals with the actors began—were held on two consecutive Saturday mornings, September 18 and 25.[5] Meanwhile, Craig himself, oblivious to most of these developments, was busy in Genoa with his own characteristically impressionistic approach to the problem of staging *The Pretenders*—an approach not ideally suited, perhaps, to a situation in which a rigorously limited two-month rehearsal schedule was expected to culminate in a finished production.

I reach out and touch a play with my left hand, as it were, and try to receive the thing through my senses, and then make some note with my right hand which will record what it is I have felt. . . . I have so often found that this sensitive way of touching a piece—when it is a real piece—is more illuminating to me than to stop and begin thinking over it at once. Thinking comes afterwards. Thinking is for practical purposes. (p. 8)

Craig goes on in *A Production* to describe a number of the many projected but unused designs which he drew in Genoa, including a series of sketches for the opening scene (one of which, providing an interesting comparison with Poulsen's proposal for the Norwegian "stave-kirk," he reproduces), two projects for Bishop Nikolas's death scene (3. 1), an expansive and colorful rendering of King Haakon's prolonged wedding feast at the beginning of the second act of the play

(see ill. 11), and a design, not reproduced, for the final mob scene in the courtyard at Elgesæter. These and numerous other projects and variants are among the forty-eight full-scale drawings and scene designs for *The Pretenders* which are to be found in the Collection Craig. Ultimately, as we shall see, Craig was obliged to adopt a greatly simplified permanent stage construction which precluded the use of any of these earlier projects.

A crisis of some sort was inevitable. The telegram despatched by William Norrie, head of the Royal Theatre, on October 2 speaks for itself: "What time can we wait you want you immediately." By this time, however, the great man had begun his journey from the tiny village of San Martino d'Albero to the Danish capital—via an elaborate route that included stopovers in Genoa, Milan, Basel, and Berlin (at the Hotel Excelsior)![6] The day before the start of rehearsals on October 7, he turned up in Copenhagen—to the astonishment of everyone—bearing what seemed to be a complete scenography for the production. "Like a bolt from a blue sky, the world-famous English theatre reformer and theatre philosopher, Edward Gordon Craig, arrived here yesterday," proclaimed one awestruck interviewer. "No one had heard that the Royal Theatre had planned to call in this most interesting of all experimenters in modern theatre art."

Craig himself chose to appear vague about the nature of his duties. "How long I shall remain here and what I shall direct or draw designs for—I hardly know yet. . . . When Johannes Poulsen is finished with his première this evening, which I shall attend, we shall begin tomorrow to discuss how we may work together on his jubilee performance." Even more enigmatic were the remarks which followed. "It is not certain that we shall simplify *The Pretenders*. At first I wanted to clear away, wash the cupboards clean. Now I want particularly to teach the actors what they have forgotten, first and foremost how to speak. I want to help the actors to re-discover a part of their art that has become lost, and I want to search out together with them some of the secrets of the theatre."[7]

Nearly two weeks of precious time were then wasted in the futile attempt to reconcile Craig's preliminary designs with the models and plans for the scenery already prepared by Thorolf Pedersen. (The curious remark by "Conrad Tower" in *The Mask*—"Mr. Craig told me that, when he arrived in Copenhagen at the beginning of October, no preliminary work had even commenced: 'Nothing was done or even prepared' "—may be taken either as evasiveness or as an instance of

wishful thinking!)[8] Craig appears to have been extremely anxious to avoid the confrontation which was bound to come. The first performance he attended at the Royal Theatre was the opening of *En dag på Hirschholm Slot* [A day at Hirschholm Castle], an elaborately staged period pastiche by the critic and playwright Sven Lange, and his letter of the same date to Johannes Poulsen, who appeared in the production, radiates a rather oily determination to play the diplomat.

I was charmed with everything—the absence of effort—the absence of pretension—and the perfect good taste. I do not know a company of sweeter ladies and gentlemen—and I do hope that *the old scenepainter* will be a noble old dear, like the rest of you, and not mind me. I come to disturb *no* one and if it disturbs the old gentleman I shall be very grieved. The talent shown in the sceneries tonight is a high one and I am sure I wish I could say so to the old gentleman personally.—He would find in me an ardent and sincere admirateur.[9]

A showdown was inevitable, however, for the "intelligent," "charming," and "excessively talented" old scene-painter was determined to squeeze both his own and Craig's sets on to "that fiendish turn-table stage" of his, and, as Craig admits with frank simplicity in *A Production*, "we were killing each other." Only Johannes Poulsen's resourceful intervention appears to have saved the day: Thorolf Pedersen pleaded ill-health and was allowed to retire from the project on a leave of absence, while Craig was, with great difficulty, persuaded to remain and take full charge of the staging and costuming. In *A Production* he makes no effort to deemphasize the immensely positive and balanced influence which Poulsen's personality exerted on his volatile temperament during these difficult weeks: "When I was in Copenhagen, he gave me a loyal and instantaneous co-operation, and he gave it all the time: in the bad times, in the very bad times,—in the middle of the catastrophic times even" (p. 11).

With less than four weeks of rehearsal time still remaining, Craig took the bold step of abandoning both Pedersen's cumbersome turn-table concept *and* all of his own preliminary ideas about a succession of changeable scenes. Instead, he eliminated the principle of successive decors entirely, in favor of a simple architectural device—a permanent structure of platforms that could be localized, in a symbolic manner, by means of projections, occasional hangings, the deployment of nonrepresentational set pieces and small panels, and the selective use of central objects expressive of a particular scene's essen-

tial idea. There was no attempt to reduplicate the large-scale movable screens of the Moscow *Hamlet*. But to anyone familiar with Craig's earlier experiments, there were very few surprises in his revised approach to *The Pretenders*. "I have only used *improvisations* on my first expressions of 1900–1906 and those earlier days," he himself admits in *The Mask*; "it would be impossible for a spectator who had seen, observingly, former productions, not to notice some relationship of work of one period with the work of another period."

It is worth reemphasizing the crucial point that the physical staging of this production, as it was finally executed, consisted *entirely* of Craig's work. The stage manager's floor plans, preserved in the Royal Theatre Library, can be compared with Craig's designs to confirm this fact. Although, for example, the detailed "Memling" sketch by Poulsen of the palace room in act 3 does figure prominently in his promptbook, both these same floor plans and Craig's own discarded rendering of the sketch (marked "done for *Pretenders* in 1926 before the change") make it abundantly clear that the idea was never actually used on the stage. Ove Christian Pedersen, son of "the old scene-painter" and a man much more responsive to the aims and methods of the New Stagecraft, took over the task of completing the scenery on the basis of Craig's revised designs and under his supervision.

Poul Nielsen, whose formidable skill as a technician earned Craig's genuine admiration ("I have seen clouds and skies before done at that horizon affair—but I have never seen it done so well")[10] worked assiduously to perfect the back projections and complicated lighting effects on which the *mise en scène* came to depend so heavily. Here as before, the creative use of light to express, in visual and symbolic terms, the inner tensions and rhythms of the drama was of paramount importance to Craig's approach. Nielsen's full script of light and sound cues for the production is found in the Royal Theatre Library, but Craig's own notes—in particular a detailed lighting plot dated November 3 and marked "as arranged for Mr Poul Nielsen"[11]—indicate that he himself also took a direct and very active part in the designing of this dimension of the production.

# CHAPTER FOUR

## REHEARSALS

Some additional time—but not enough—was gained when the opening of *The Pretenders* was postponed from the original target date of November 9, the actual anniversary of the Poulsen brothers' debut, to November 14. A perusal of the theatre's daily Journal affords a good impression of the nature of the rehearsal difficulties that confronted the production. Even this postponement allowed for a total of only thirty-four rehearsals, including the two initial "scenery rehearsals" held in September before Craig's arrival. A complete run-through, with music, supernumeraries, and lighting and sound cues in place, could not be scheduled until November 8, and even then it proved impossible to reach the fifth act.

The first completed run-through of the production, held two days later, lasted from 11:30 A.M. until six in the evening. Under normal circumstances, the final dress rehearsal on the day before the opening would have had the character of a completely finished *generalprøve*, to which the press and a select audience would have been invited. In this case, however, "there was no admittance to the rehearsal. After the rehearsal, individual things were repeated again until 5:30 P.M.," the keeper of the theatre's Journal records tersely. Something of the nature of these "individual things" and of the difficulties in general that still beset the production can be gathered from the copious notes which Craig took the previous day, and which are reproduced in the Appendix to this study. Under the circumstances, of course, any further postponement of the Poulsen jubilee would have been out of

the question. Tickets for the much-awaited opening had gone on sale on the morning of November 12, at double prices and with a limit of three to a customer, and all available seats were taken within a matter of hours.

For our purposes, it is obviously of special interest to gauge, insofar as it is possible to do so, the nature of Craig's involvement in these rehearsals. Clearly, it would seem, his own assertion in *A Production* that he "ended up designing the whole play, and, with the assistance of Johannes, directing all the rehearsals" (p. 6) stands in need of some modification. A nine-page typescript in the Collection Craig, apparently the original version of the "Conrad Tower" interview in *The Mask*, contains the following remark that did not find its way into print. "No, I do not conceive and control the whole production in every detail, that would take me 5–6 months. We run along as best we can and make the most of a short time." Ulla Poulsen Skou recalls that "eventually Gordon Craig also participated actively in rehearsals with the cast. Despite language difficulties, he was able to follow the work of the actors and to make changes when he found it necessary to do so."[1] As early as October 21, *Politiken* was able to report that "Gordon Craig is present at all rehearsals, in addition to which he is painting the scenery and also designing the costumes."

We may perhaps imagine Craig of a morning at work on his designs, ensconced in quarters at the Hotel d'Angleterre that had been converted to a kind of field command post crammed with books and cluttered with scene drawings and models. "With the commence-ment of rehearsal at eleven-thirty," recalls a distinctly disenchanted Svend Johansen, who as a young designer was assigned by the theatre to assist the great visitor in his labors. "Craig would rush, like a second Raphael, across the square in his long flowing overcoat, wearing-an enormous hat that had to serve as a temporary halo, and surrounded by a flock of helpers."[2] As colorful as the presence of Craig and his acolytes at rehearsals must have been, meanwhile, his role in the actual directorial process was confined largely to that of critic and adviser to Poulsen, who retained control of this aspect of the production. In Copenhagen as at so many other junctures in his career, Craig's uncompromising vision of a sovereign master-director and his disdainful insistence that *"it is impossible for a work of art ever to be produced where more than one brain is permitted to direct"*[3] were lofty principles that were, however, inevitably tempered by the self-evident realities of the practical situation at hand.

At the front of his own interleaved "book" for the play, Craig has painstakingly pasted in a lengthy newspaper clipping which, in an elliptical but nonetheless very revealing way, illustrates his personal view of his directorial contribution to *The Pretenders*. This clipping, entitled "Marshal Foch's Way" and published a day or two after November 11, recounts an Armistice Day interview with Foch, who reminisces about his role as commander-in-chief in the First World War—and with whose circumstances (*and* rank!) Craig obviously seems to have identified completely. "I have never commanded in the way that is popularly thought," Foch is reported as saying. "What I did was to bring those around me to my ideas, and that is very different."

The field marshal goes on to describe his strategy to persuade the allied leaders, Pershing, Haig, and Pétain, to follow his plan of attack in the crucial summer of 1918—and here Craig has outlined the relevant passage in red. "I might have replied by giving a categoric order. But that was not my way. I know that orders are badly carried out when they are received unwillingly. I preferred to assume the role of an adviser rather than that of commander-in-chief." By these means, Foch (read Craig) "persuaded everybody, by pride, by logic, or merely by sense of responsibility, to rally to my views. And everything went off much better than if I had simply imposed my authority." Craig found even more striking "allegorical" significance in Foch's actions during the bleak days of November, 1914, when he succeeded in dissuading the Allies from abandoning the lines of the Yser and thereby risking the wholesale annihilation of their troops. "Then I had not a piece of paper in my pocket appointing me commander-in-chief. I did not even command the French army. I was merely a French general. . . . Not orders, but merely advice. But I had persuaded both the British field-marshal and the King of the Belgians that the advice was good and they gave their orders accordingly [that is, to give up the retreat and stand firm]. And I think that there, where I had no right to command, I really did command."[4] At this juncture in his career at least, Craig saw in the Foch story a perfect and consoling image of his own curiously ambiguous position, as a theatre commander with neither an army nor a commission.

Nevertheless, the collaboration between Poulsen and Craig remained a vigorous and fruitful one. On those evenings when the actor was not appearing on stage, he would visit Craig's hotel room in order to go over the material for the next day's rehearsal, elicit his sugges-

tions and ideas, and rehearse his own part under Craig's personal supervision. (In the Danish actor's own view, the whole process of rehearsal represented the most significant and most satisfying aspect of the performer's art. "As far as I am concerned, rehearsals constitute the most valuable and the best part of my work as an actor," he later declared in an article for the newspaper *Dagens Nyheder* [December 17, 1933]. "It is a wonderful sensation to feel how a character emerges with greater and greater strength out of the dead print, how it acquires shape and color, and how one's own inner self gradually comes to resemble the figure one has been imagining.") Accordingly, Poulsen's promptbook for *The Pretenders* is filled with alternate proposals, question marks, and even the occasional direction in English, all of which suggest Craig's influence at work. Interpretational notes for the part of Bishop Nikolas predominate, and in this sense the document is as much an actor's role copy, reflecting the results of these face-to-face "rehearsals" with Craig, as it is a director's "book" for the play.

For Craig, Poulsen mirrored an ideal—molded in the image of Henry Irving—of immense versatility and sovereign craftsmanship that inspired his unqualified admiration. "This is an actor—one who, on any stage and at any time, in Opera, Ballet, Farce, Tragedy, in all of it—can attain the chief thing, the essence, dramatic life—and who can speak to us by some few but powerful means," he wrote to Haagen Falkenfleth, editor of *Nationaltidende*, on the occasion of Poulsen's fiftieth birthday in 1931.[5] As we know, Craig had no patience with an imprecise or uncritical acting interpretation. "*Broad—sharp cut—clear,*" reads a remark in a small notebook, marked "Copenhagen 1926" on its cover and preserved in the Bibliothèque Nationale:

The great actor is the only one who does what we call *designer* work— (measure)—the design may be hidden under a hundred natural details—*but the design is there.*
  Lemaître—Talma—Petrolini—Terravilla—Irving

This typically aphoristic notation calls to mind Craig's earliest strictures on the cult of impersonation ("this idea of reproducing Nature") in acting—"the bringing of excessive gesture, swift mimicry, speech which bellows and scene which dazzles, on to the stage, in the wild and vain belief that by such means vitality can be conjured there"—and his attendant admonition that "it is bad art to make so

personal, so emotional, an appeal that the beholder forgets the thing itself while swamped by the personality, the emotion, of its maker."[6] To Johannes Poulsen he wrote bluntly in 1930: "Never forget that you are very robust and that your *quiet voice* and *subtle gestures* are your strongest helpers. No one can speak more quietly and more delicately than you—so remember."[7]

Presumably he was less frank and open with the Danish director and his cast concerning his own true opinion of the tone and quality of Ibsen's drama in general (at last insofar as he was able to judge it from Farquharson Sharp's Everyman translation): "Say what you will its a preachy play—rightwrong I hear the sanctimonious voice—voices—for nearly all of 'em turn on the tap/ and one can understand Tchekov's smiling impatience with Ibsen." This disenchanted assessment of *The Pretenders*, inscribed across the title page of Craig's script, is reechoed often enough in his private papers to cause one to wonder about the wisdom of his having agreed to stage it in the first place. Elsewhere in the same script, for example, one meets the following "Nietzschean" declaration. "For my part I find that this tragedy (& this kind of piece) is too weighed down by reasonableness & not enlightened by art for representation of it to be of much worth." (Within a very few years, of course, Craig was ready to commit his disenchantment with Ibsen to print in his book on Irving. "I have had moments of emancipation when I felt that there was nobody so splendid as Ibsen—until I emancipated myself still further, and discovered that Shakespeare beat him hollow on his own ground—and that there was still another land or two farther south, and a civilization or two farther east."[8]

In Copenhagen, Craig seems to have become increasingly frustrated not only by the play but also by the inevitable practical exigencies of the rehearsal process itself. At the end of the fourth act, after the street battle in Oslo, Craig's copy of the play contains a long, exasperated aside:

This awful cutting was done when only 3 weeks remained to get the play ready & 150 *rehearsals needed* & impossible to have.

Then came Johannes P. & proposed wholesale cutting.

Rehearsals only possible from 10 or 9 in the morning to 5:30 evening—after which the play of the night had to be set on the stage & at 6:30 the actors begin to get ready for the show at 7 or 7:30, I forget which. The stagehands hardly had any rest either.

Unlike this comment, which has obviously been penned after the fact, a few pieces of evidence can be found which shed light upon a more significant matter—namely, the nature and extent of Craig's actual contributions *during* the rehearsal process. The most complete of these, the transcription of his "notes made rapidly in the dark about the small errors to be put right" after the penultimate dress rehearsal, is printed in full in the Appendix. A considerably earlier—and in a sense an even more revealing—document is a scene-by-scene list of comments which he dispatched to Johannes Poulsen following a long rehearsal on November 1. Craig himself evidently considered these notes important enough to make a transcription of them, labeled "copy of letter to Poulsen to brace him up to better things" and carefully preserved in the Collection Craig. For our purposes, these comments provide an unusual glimpse of Craig at work during rehearsals—functioning, it may be added, more as a critical adviser or an enlightened connoisseur than as a creative director of actors. (Ibsen's own act and scene divisions have been inserted in brackets in the following excerpt.)

The result of a rush up to Nov. 1 [The letter which Poulsen received opens more diplomatically. "This piece—summed up the result so far is—"]
Scene 1 [1. 1]: Begins well—almost good but for the acting of Inga, Hakon, etc., which has to be finer.
Scene 2 [1. 2]: *Little Room.*—bad—nothing.
Scene 3 [1. 2]: *Baldachino*—not so bad—but needs finer, closer, *neater* acting.
Scene 4 [2. 1]: Banquet Hakon. Poor—except for Bishop.
Scene 5 [3. 1]: Bishops Death. Good—but needs cutting more and better accompaniments. *Storm—Statisten* etc.
Scene 6 [?]: Is scene 6 necessary? [Poulsen's letter reads, "Now cut out—Bishop on bier."]
Scene 7 [3. 2]: Bedroom.—Needs better acting—richer lighting—pace & quiet.
Scene 8 [4. 1]: Skule Banquet. I want to see and hear it. Scenes poor up to now—*more beauty in this*. [Poulsen's letter reads, "Acting, movement, scenes all must be the scene of *Beauty*."]
Scene 9, 10 [4. 2; 5. 1]: Needs pace and quieter—at present a little *vague*.
Scene 11 [5. 2]: Bishops ghost. More terror & pace—*slow*—scene allright.
Scene 12 [5. 3]: Scene poor so far. *Acting* can be immense, at present poor. Scene and lighting nothing so far.
We are going along allright but we are going too fast. Your cutting is

wonderfully *good;* but can not we cut more, can we cut a whole scene or even two? [Compare this with Craig's disgruntled remarks on cutting cited above!] Can we not take some scenes more *rapidly* and quietly.

I would almost like to accompany *the whole* of *Skule Banquet* with music—to keep it beautiful and support the actors. Except for 1st. moment of Act I and your death-scene nothing is ELECTRICAL.

Ever devotedly

yours

G.C.[9]

While, as this instructive document indicates, Craig took only an indirect role in rehearsing the Royal Theatre cast, contributing to the process chiefly through advice and exhortations communicated to Johannes Poulsen, he eagerly adopted a much more active role in the prolonged late-night technical rehearsals that the demanding *mise en scène* required. At such rehearsals, Poulsen's widow recalls, Craig took his place at the director's desk in the auditorium and rehearsed and refined the complicated lightning plot, while her husband walked through the various movements and positions of his cast on the stage.

I sat a little apart from Gordon Craig and observed him. The light from the lamp over the desk glinted in his glasses as he looked quickly up at the stage after having made his notations. He issued instructions to the stage manager and the chief electrician, and screens were moved, platforms shifted, until the result satisfied him. . . . It was a fascinating spectacle, but the deepest impression was made by Gordon Craig's fierce involvement in every detail of the process which was taking place.[10]

Not unexpectedly, then, it was chiefly in terms of the coordination and balance of the scenographic composition—the dynamic interplay of lighting effects, scenic objects, groupings, costumes, and the line and color of the stage space itself—that Craig sought to formulate his response to the challenge of *The Pretenders.* True to his principles, the primary objectives of his design concept were simplification and suggestion. "The greatest surprise he brings us is his extraordinarily great simplicity," Johannes Poulsen declared in a front-page interview on the eve of the opening.

He has cut out every superficial element with respect to scenery and staging—and thereby he has made the actors the principal focus.

It is easy to make *The Pretenders* into an extravaganza, he says, and both he [?] and others have done that before. Now he insists that audiences are never

34

better entertained than when they are allowed to collaborate, and therefore we must only guide their imagination.

A child who is given a match-box can make a wonderful locomotive out of it, if we help his imagination to get started. An expensive metal locomotive, ready to run at once, is not nearly as much fun.

When we sit as spectators in a theatre, we are all children, Gordon Craig insists—and now we shall see if he is right.[11]

In order to comprehend and assess more fully the implementation of Craig's ideas in actual practice, it remains for us to look more closely at those source documents and items of iconographic evidence that can aid in recapturing, to some degree at least, the effect which his last important work for the stage produced upon the audiences who witnessed one of the sixteen performances of this unique experiment. Visionary comments and pithy propositions abound both in his published remarks and unpublished notes on the staging of *The Pretenders*.

Some scenes are static & at rest (so that the scenery must be so).
Some scenes shift & change (let the scenery dance attendance).
Let the changing ones come & go *in bits*.[12]

Yet, until such statements as these are measured and reassessed in terms of the factual realities of the theatrical event itself, they tell us at best only half the story.

# CHAPTER FIVE

## THEORY IN PRACTICE:

## CRAIG'S SCENOGRAPHY

Upon entering the Royal Theatre auditorium on November 14, 1926, an observant spectator would have noticed at once one of the most striking and—in view of Craig's repeated rejection of any suggestion of historical "authenticity"—most unexpected features of his scenography: a Gobelin-like front curtain showing an impressionistic rendering of an ancient map of medieval Scandinavia. "In a library in Florence," Poulsen declared with enthusiasm in the interview cited earlier, "Gordon Craig has discovered an old map of Scandinavia—Denmark, Norway, and Sweden—as it was during the period in which Ibsen has placed *The Pretenders*, the middle of the thirteenth century—or rather, as Scandinavia was thought to be."

In fact, despite his lofty public dismissals of the importance of historical period and place in the play, Craig seems to have devoted a good deal of thought to these very matters. His interleaved script is filled with such items as a drawing of eleventh-century bells "suspended on a rod, struck with hammers," prescriptions for medieval costumes to be "coloured as illuminated ms. of Psalter-Canterbury" ("To Copenhagen archives and library to find the exact colours," he adds in a note), and a sketch of the front curtain labeled "old Norway map . . . in Florence I found it & used it." This much-publicized "tableau curtain" device, with its uncharacteristic gesture toward a definition of historical time and place, was closed occasionally to

facilitate the more complicated scene changes without having to "condescend" to the Reinhardt alternative of a turntable stage. In *A Production* he even records (unverifiable) timings for the various changes, in order to reemphasize his success in this respect.[1]

Undoubtedly Craig's best scene was the familiar design for the splendid opening of the play in the churchyard of Christ Church in Bergen, in which a crowd outside the church eagerly awaits the outcome of the ordeal with the white-hot iron that will confirm the birthright of Inga's son, Haakon Haakonsson. No realistic Norwegian stave-church loomed in the background. Instead, writes Svend Borberg, "the curtain rises and we see a forest of lances grow toward the sky, while behind them, projected on a cyclorama: a dream in yellow light and bluish shadow, a half-dematerialized cathedral."[2]

To others, it seemed as if the divine choice of Haakon was "embodied by the stylized lines of light that hover in the sky and resemble both church arches and the northern lights: it is as though signs are seen in sun and moon that God himself has spoken."[3] "We are at once removed from the usual theatre gothicism," agreed Christian Gulman *(Berlingske Tidende)*. "No painted church as a background for Meininger processions, but a beautifully effaced impression of high columns of light, and a forest of lances above the richly colorful warriors—a square in Florence rather than a picture of medieval Norway." The "Florentine" color harmonies which many of the critics found so noticeable represent, here as elsewhere in Craig's work, a basic element in the theatre artist's vision of a scene. "He first of all chooses certain colours which seem to him to be in harmony with the spirit of the play, rejecting other colours as out of tune."[4]

Craig's papers abound with notes concerning chromatic selection and on the flyleaf of Poulsen's promptbook one finds a short list—half in English, half in Danish!—specifying the four color values (chosen from six possibilities) with which Craig sought to reveal the spirit of Ibsen's drama: blue (crossed over), gold, "dirty white," violet, black (crossed over), cardinal. In the finished scene design (ill. 4), the interplay of these basic color values is clearly in evidence in the impressive tableau—though in Craig's *Pretenders* one lacks the sense of as clear and logical a link between his color scheme and the work itself as in the case of, say, the two colors he proposes for *Macbeth* ("one for the rock, the man; one for the mist, the spirit").[5]

The rather impressionistic figure composition in Craig's churchyard design is usefully amplified by two rough but quite detailed

explanatory drawings of it (each a little different in its arrangement, both presumably sketched by Poulsen) in the promptbook (see ill. 5). From these drawings and the supplementary evidence of a surviving costume list, we can gain a more exact idea of the immensity of the stage crowd required by the scene. Two serpentine groups of supernumeraries flank the towering church portal on either side: a long curving line of sixteen Birkebeiners, the "Birchlegs" who are Haakon's supporters, on the stage-right side is balanced by a correspondingly curved line of twelve of Skule's men opposite them. Behind the Birkebeiners, one would have glimpsed clusters of eight apprentices, fourteen or fifteen citizens, and, nearest to the ramp of stairs leading up to the gigantic "doorway" (actually a projection effect) in which Bishop Nikolas and later Inga appear, four boys. The opposite side of the stage was balanced by comparable knots of extras: four boys, seventeen peasant women, and another cluster of twenty-eight knights and supporters of Skule and the two (somewhat superfluous) minor pretenders to the throne, Sigurd Ribbung and Guthorm Ingesson. In the foreground of this imposing tableau the principal antagonists in the drama were arranged: Haakon, joined by the chaplain Ivar Bodde, Vegard Væradal, and the faithful Dagfinn the Peasant, and his rival Earl Skule, seconded by Gregorius Jonsson and Paul Flida. Hence, at the electric moment that is illustrated by Craig's design, as Inga appears before the amazed crowd on the church steps ("God has judged. Look at these hands; with them have I borne the white-hot iron") more than a hundred and ten actors would have filled the spacious stage of the Royal Theatre.[6]

From beginning to end, the taut, emotional opening scene of Ibsen's drama was charged with the expansive visual theatricality which had become the hallmark of Johannes Poulsen's earlier, Reinhardt-inspired productions. Both his copiously annotated promptbook and Nielsen's "signal book" of light and sound cues are filled with the complicated beat-by-beat instructions on which the dynamic *mise en scène* depended. (Craig's own papers—especially the rehearsal notes reproduced in the Appendix—help chiefly to balance the picture by indicating what went wrong.) Craig's first stage picture came to life with dramatic suddenness. "Chess men! Still group at first—then wake up at a clap of a hand," he himself remarks in preplanning notes, and Poulsen's detailed promptbook instructions indicate how this idea was put into practice. "The curtain rises—all dark, spotlight in on the center, the spot grows in rings, larger and

4. Design by Gordon Craig for the opening scene
of *The Pretenders*. (From Craig, *A Production*)

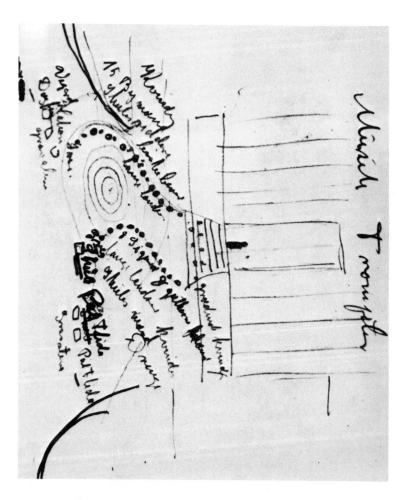

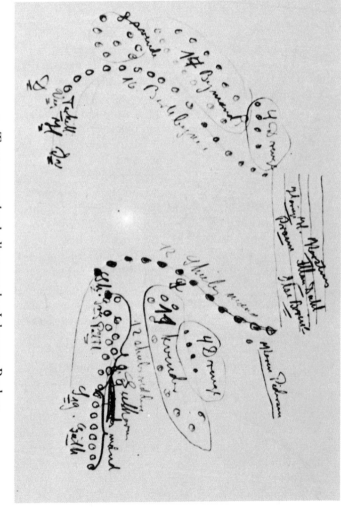

5. Two promptbook diagrams by Johannes Poulsen
for the opening scene of *The Pretenders*.
(Royal Theatre Library)

larger, until the bells begin to ring, distantly and gradually louder. Next comes the slide projection of the church, and then the bigger bells—the people who have been standing completely still now begin to move—then Skule speaks: 'What keeps them so long in there?' "

As this promptbook excerpt also reveals, the skillful orchestration of sounds—of bells, of trumpet-pierced psalms and glorias, of music from a mighty organ (strategically positioned in the green-room)—contributed greatly to the desired emotional effect. The sixteen nuns and twelve priests and monks who appeared behind Bishop Nikolas inside the church were all singers in the opera chorus. Even so relatively unmoved a critic as Cavling declared in *Politiken* that "the English director deserves an unqualified compliment for the accompanying music and choral singing backstage; it reached the audience as a delicate, subtle undercurrent, a distant hum that had a captivating effect." As the singing from inside the church increases in volume following Haakon's first declaration of his unyielding self-confidence, Poulsen's promptcopy notes that "the women and half of the citizens—some of Skule's warriors and some apprentices fall on their knees." A beat later, as the Chaplain prays for Inga's safety ("Christ protect your innocent hands, mother of the King"), the remainder of the crowd was directed to kneel, with the exception of the four pretenders and the twenty-eight men holding long lances. (Of the latter, Craig notes "spears to sway on and back" in a large, untidy sketchbook containing scattered observations on this scene, adding, "Two spears *shorter* across to hold crowd to be moved rapidly.") Skule's wistful line, "Did she scream? Has she dropped the iron?" was supplied with a direct motivation by Poulsen: "a scream, half stifled, from a woman up in the crowd who is taken ill/ all turn round and look at her." (Craig was skeptical of this effect. "The scream is stupid—it should be a *slight* cry," he remarks in his dress-rehearsal notes.)

The tensely awaited entrance of Haakon's mother, Inga from Varteig, represented a critical turning point in the scene. ("Inga must bear with more ceremony," reads a grumpish remark in Craig's sketchbook; even at the penultimate dress rehearsal, he felt obliged to note that "Inga not to look like the witches in *Macbeth*—she is a queen.") At her appearance in the church doorway ("no head covering only grey brushed-back hair"), the promptbook directs that "all fall on their knees, including the lancers, only [Eyvind Johan-] Svendsen [as Haakon] and Adam [Poulsen, as Skule] remain standing."

The atmosphere of feverish, almost hypnotic religious fanaticism with which Johannes Poulsen endeavored to surround Inga's "miracle" was steadily intensified. When voices from the crowd describe her hands ("They are as fair and white as before"), everyone is "all the way down on the ground and now begins to crawl up toward her." As the entire crowd calls out, "He is truly Haakon Sverresson's heir," a sudden change takes place, "the entire populace up—in most extreme excitement embracing one another, swinging with whatever they have." The feverish climate of the scene reached its highest pitch a moment later: on Paul Flida's (trebly emphasized) remark that "doubt whispered through every cottage in the land," the stage became a seething, gyrating mass of movement that swirled in the background while the triumphant Haakon confronted his frustrated rivals.

Before leaving this initial scene, one additional salient feature of Craig's compositional technique invites comment. As might be expected, this production set out to alter completely the more traditional approach to the play taken by its previous director, Julius Lehmann, in 1899. Hence, a comparison of the stage manager's records of these two productions (see ills. 6 and 7) is extremely instructive. One very obvious change is, of course, the development from painted, illusionistic scenery in 1899—namely the church construction in the background and the cut drop placed at the fourth wing position in the plan to create perspective—to the use of an abstract, three-dimensional structure coupled with slide projections in 1926. Another—less obvious and possibly less advantageous— change was the abandonment of a relatively open and neutral playing area *surrounded* by scenery in the older approach, where a wall, some bushes (marked 5 and 6 on the floor plan), and "7 new grave crosses" (3) were distributed around the perimeter of the acting space. By contrast, the plan for Craig's stage is completely filled by a cluttered, layer-cake profusion of platforms, abstract shapes, and objects, including "22 new gravestones" (marked 3 on the floor plan) and the ubiquitous "new grey set-pieces used in all acts and scenes" which litter the forestage—but which remain deceptively out of sight in Craig's published design.

Following its "prologue" in the churchyard of Christ Church, Ibsen's drama moves indoors and—apart from a brief battle in the streets of Oslo at the close of the fourth act—remains there until the final two scenes of the play. The struggle between crippling self-doubt and supreme self-assurance is played out to its inevitable end

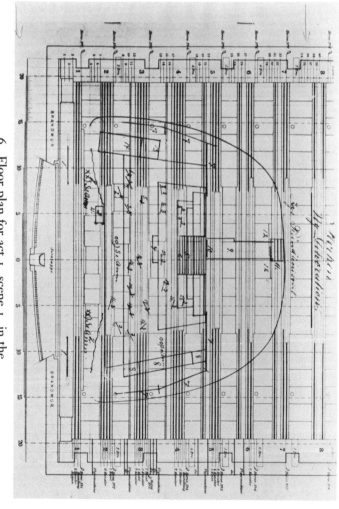

6. Floor plan for act 1, scene 1, in the
1926 production. (Royal Theatre Library)

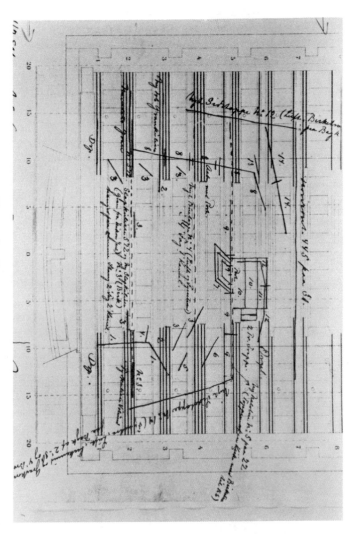

7. Floor plan for act 1, scene 1,
as staged by Julius Lehmann in 1899.
(Royal Theatre Library)

8. Design project by Gordon Craig for
act 1, scene 2. *"Positively not* a carpet bazaar."
(From Craig, *A Production*)

within the confines of a succession of politically charged historical arenas: Haakon's palace in Bergen, the episcopal residence and the palace of King Skule in Oslo, and finally the palace at Nidaros.

The problem of designing the play's multiple interiors proved to be Craig's severest challenge and the source of much of the critical dissatisfaction with his scenography. On the one hand, the permanent presence of a structure of nonrepresentational shapes and platforms in the background seemed, to many observers, awkward and obtrusive. On the other hand, in his determination to avoid, at all costs, "any attempt to show the spectators an exact view of some historical period of architecture," Craig seemed to be sacrificing all sense of stylistic consistency. "The settings represented a styleless mixture," declared one of the more dissatisfied of the production's critics, "some recalled medieval manuscript illuminations with their symbolic suggestion of locality, some were cubist and others Reinhardt-like in style, while some were semi-naturalistic."[7] A closer examination of several of Craig's "interiors" for *The Pretenders* may help to shed clearer light on the problem to which such criticism refers.

Craig's simplest stage pictures were often his most evocative in this production. It quickly became obvious, for instance, that the unwieldy "carpet bazaar" design for act 1, scene 2, which he had brought with him to Copenhagen (ill. 8)—the palace hall where Haakon, as Craig says, "signs so many documents and practically banishes to far-off spots those who are so very dear to him"—was incompatible with his revised concept of a single architectural grouping of platforms and movable panels. Accordingly, he dispensed entirely with scenery and instead divided the scene into two principal actions, for each of which he chose one object as a visible sign of its idea. For the portion of the scene during which Skule's wife, his daughter, and his sister anxiously watch the royal election from the window, he placed a tentlike "Ladies' Pavilion" on an otherwise bare stage. "The rest of us would have shown the whole room, with its walls and with the window as a central point," declared Poulsen. "Gordon Craig shows us, in the spirit of the great painters of the Middle Ages, only the window, which is what the scene is about, while the rest of the stage stands empty."[8] (However, neither this comment nor the design shown in illustration 9 reveals the interesting fact that Craig actually placed a second, smaller pavilion beside the larger one, in which a peasant woman sat humming "one sad song and one gay song" as she worked at a spinning-wheel.)

9. Revised design by Gordon Craig
for act 1, scenes 2 and 3.
(From Craig, *A Production*)

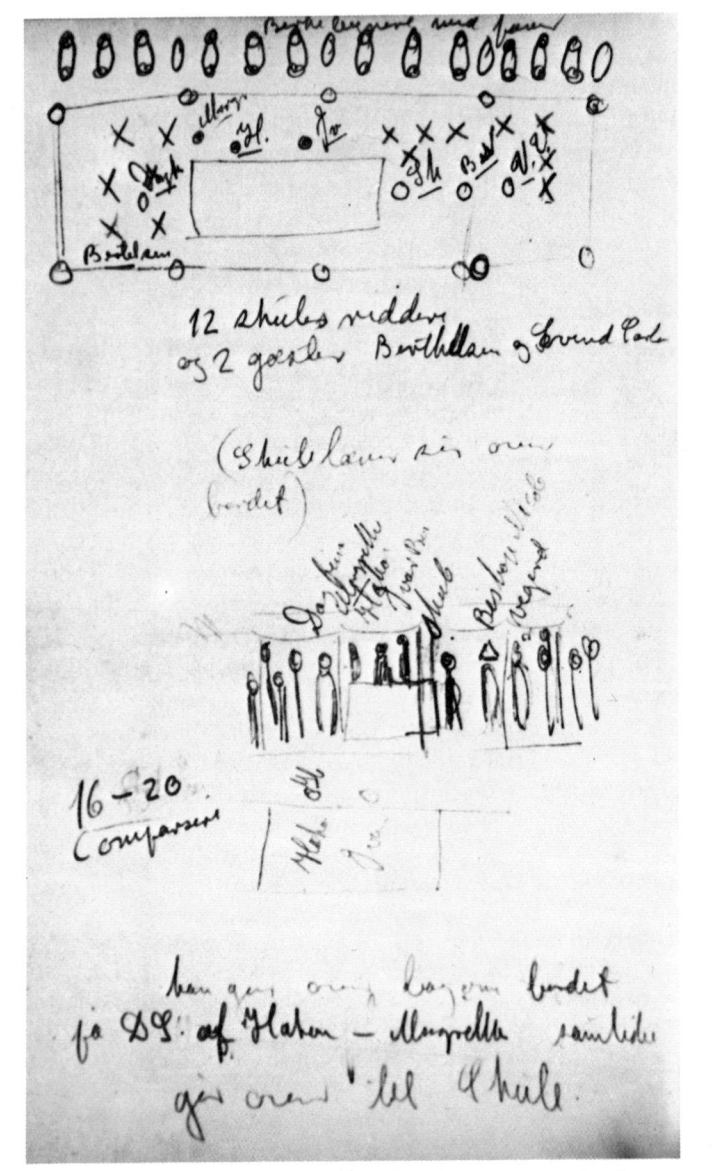

10. Details from Johannes Poulsen's promptbook
for act 1, scenes 2 and 3 ("16-20 extras").
(Royal Theatre Library)

To accommodate the second part of Ibsen's scene—the council meeting in which King Haakon seems to act so rashly—Craig conceived the simple expedient of a portable baldachin, as seen in illustrations 9 and 10, supported by ten gilded posts and carried in elaborate procession by pages. With everyone in the scene remaining within the confines of the canopy, the resulting constriction of movement conveyed, in the designer's terms, the "stiffness of a crowded ceremonial meeting."[9] Poulsen's ground plan, seen side by side with Craig's sketch, conveys a clear impression of the kind of positioning which the designer had in mind.

Not all of the production's interior scenes displayed the same degree of clarity and symbolic simplicity, however. Haakon's council meeting was followed, without the act break which is in Ibsen's text, by the marathon wedding feast celebrating the marriage of King Haakon to Skule's daughter, Margrete, during which her father and Bishop Nikolas conspire over a game of chess. The promptbook describes the scene change which, according to Craig, required only sixty-five seconds to execute, in detail. "The curtain closes. Ladies' pavilion and baldacin [sic] are removed. The light now changes at a single stroke to become yellowish red on the cyclorama (autumn sunset). The gilded panels and throne and chairs are carried in."

The scene with which Craig now confronted his audience stirred up widespread confusion and disagreement. (Alone the extensiveness of his own dress-rehearsal notes on this scene suggest something of its problematic character.) On the one hand, Craig's staunchest critical advocate in the Danish press was prepared to assert that

the plastic beauty of the stage composition was clear and powerful—up to the right the royal couple, placed highest with large banners behind them, with their backs to the malice and the gossip—Nikolas, Skule, and their men, again divided into two groups, sat with their backs to each other, so that they did not always have to hear one another's speeches—thus, an elevation along a diagonal line in the stage space, running from common quarrels, through vicious intrigues, up to the untouchable power of royalty. From this composition alone one was made to realize that Haakon was and would remain king.[10]

Although one might perhaps admire its critical ingenuity, however, this glowing assessment mirrors nothing of Craig's actual intent here, which is shaped by his attitude toward Haakon as someone who "must *play* the king and overdo it." In fact, most critics reacted in a very different and much less positive manner to the curiously stylized

scene. "The castle hall where Earl Skule conducts his dark negotiations with his evil genius, the unscrupulous, crafty, and almost satanic Bishop Nikolas has an open sky for a roof and is furnished with rectangular boxes upholstered with gold foil," declared the critic for *Aftenbladet* in disgust, while *B.T.* found the scenery "oddly reminiscent of the building-blocks that children are given at Christmastime."

It seems clear that Craig was determined to impose a distorted, virtually expressionistic quality on this scene which most observers found incongruous with Ibsen's text. The substance of the banquet itself was reduced to two-dimensional cartoons of flowers and food which were attached to the low screens. "Each screen seemed to be holding heavy baskets of fruit, bottles, glasses and other Café de la Paix affairs of state," he declares in *A Production*. For the exchange between Nikolas and the credulous Skule, Craig's dress-rehearsal notes reveal that he wanted "the lights to change—and change again—to green, purple and blue on screens at back, but remain warm colour [that is, yellowish red] on front." The characters themselves are described in his interleaved script of the play as "*Mad!* & a bit drunk after several nights of feasting." "Adam Poulsen did it well," he adds as an afterthought.

It is important to realize that Craig's more bizarre scenographic ideas—in this case the interpretation of Haakon's rather conventional wedding banquet as the grotesquely flat and nightmarish feast of a cardboard king (with unmistakable family resemblances to the gilded court scene in the Moscow *Hamlet*)—were usually dictated by his own rather eccentric opinions of Ibsen's play and especially of its two principal characters, Haakon and Skule. The following comparison—a slightly reorganized but otherwise faithful presentation of Craig's notes in his interleaved play copy—reveals his personal prejudices plainly enough. According to this series of contrasts, the vascillating and self-destructive Skule, "God's stepchild on earth," now becomes the amiably disorganized and smiling seeker of truth (that is, Craig?). Haakon, the charismatic and undoubting believer in his own heroic destiny, is now viewed as a disagreeably goal-oriented, "up-tight," and beady-eyed success machine (that is, Reinhardt!). Admittedly, this painfully superficial schema, with its dashes of Bergson and traces of Nietzsche, tells us more about Craig's pet aversions and private frustrations than it does about his faculties as a literary critic. Nevertheless, his rather topsy-turvy

view of the play's complex thematic fabric had an unmistakeable effect on a number of scenes in the production, much to the dismay of the Danish critics.

| SKULE | HAAKON |
|---|---|
| Often *stops* & is seen to be squinnying up his eyes—with head raised as though looking for something. | His eyes are *round, open* & *fixed*. His body rigid except at the *end*. |
| *Autocratic*—the old kind—big lord no organizer, not shopkeeper. | He is an organizer—he will control things. |
| No *contempt* for others but often does not see them. | |
| Never nods—*leans an ear to attend* but often is not attending to what is being said. | Nods when he answers. |
| *Smiles very often*—humours of course p. 64 [that is, 3. 2, Haakon-Skule scene, "We two must share alike."] | Rarely smiles, when he does it is grim and unfriendly. |
| He suspects that a *fixed purpose* is little for a man. | Stupid *because a man of purpose*—going straight on—convinced. |
| He wishes to understand & taste the whole of life. | |
| He is a sensualist & he is good at personal combat. | |
| His dress is loose. | Dressed neatly and tightly. |
| Eyes wide apart—fine nose—regular voice—red hair— | Snobnose. Dot-like eyes—straight eyebrows—mouth ditto. Sharp, snappy voice. |
| Mirabeau—Strindberg—Garibaldi | Cavour—Hindenburg |
| *Personality*, not *system*. | System, not personality. |

Ultimately, it is the relevant pictorial evidence that aids us most in understanding the reasons for the failure of this particular scene in the theatre. Craig had created an elaborate banquet-scene design in Genoa (ill. 11), only to dispense with it in favor of a system of nine screens which were, he urges, "easily put in place and easily moved." A glance at the stage manager's floor plan (ill. 12) reveals, meanwhile,

11. Design by Gordon Craig for
Haakon's wedding banquet, staged as act 1, scene 4.
(From Craig, *A Production*)

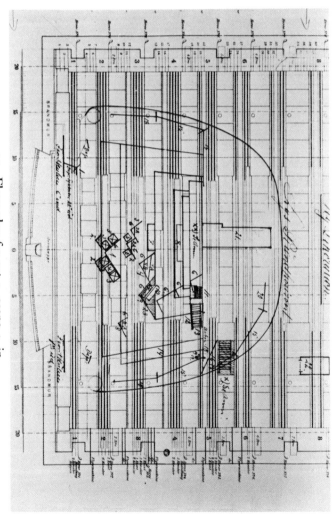

12. Floor plan for act 1, scene 4, in the 1926 production. (Royal Theatre Library)

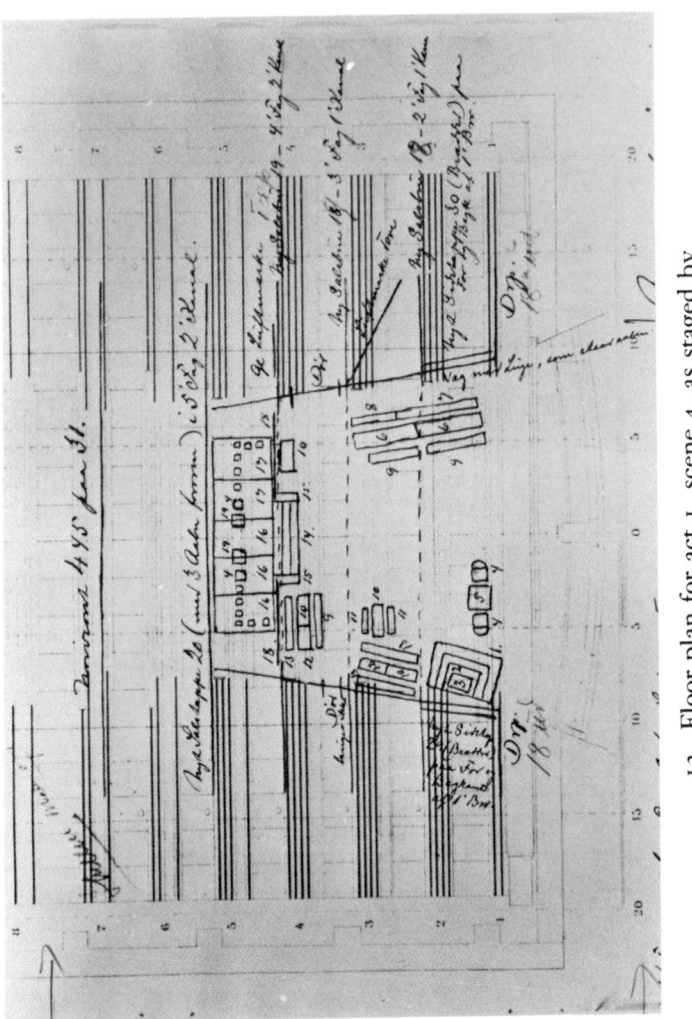

13. Floor plan for act 1, scene 4, as staged by
Julius Lehmann in 1899. (Royal Theatre Library)

that this scene, as it was actually produced, was anything but simplified in character and in fact seems to have retained many, if not all, of the characteristics of the original design. Flags and banners filled the upstage left corner of the stage. The nine low, gold-covered panels (marked 6 on the floor plan) were arranged to create the same angular positions and stacked, crowded groupings that are evident in Craig's published sketch. Scrutiny of the comparable ground plan for the 1899 production reveals some significant differences (see ill. 13). The nineteenth-century rendering of this kind of traditional banquet scene involved no less complex a stage composition, but it was one in which balance and focus were preserved without the damaging sacrifice of either a sense of proportion or a central area in which to act.

Two additional pieces of iconographic evidence, in the form of actual newspaper illustrations of this scene (see ills. 14 and 15) help to refine this comparison between old and new. The first of these pictures, a drawing by Fritz Ahlgrensson published in *Illustreret Tidende* in 1871, depicts the banquet scene as it was originally presented in Fru Heiberg's production; the sketch captures the moment when an angry Haakon returns to challenge Skule's allegiance ("Earl Skule, who is king in Norway?"). The decor—a new design painted by Gyllich for the occasion—invites comparison with the pictorial solidity of Wergmann's convent yard setting. Clearly, nothing could be further, in spirit and in style, from Craig's ideas. The second picture is a rather obviously posed photograph of Craig's own scene, published in *København* and corresponding in every detail to the floor plan. Although unfortunately very poor in quality, this photograph reveals clearly enough the disproportion, the feeling of clutter, and the clash of styles in the setting, the costuming, and the acting that critics found so distracting. (Perhaps it did not help matters that Ahlgrensson's sketch was reproduced in the program for the Craig-Poulsen production!)

Throughout Craig's scenography, an inexplicable penchant for overelaboration is sometimes startlingly at odds with his efforts to simplify and stylize. For example, the plain palace room in act 3, scene 2, which, both in Ibsen's text and in the 1899 ground plan, contains simply a bench, chairs, and "a cradle in which the royal child sleeps," was transformed in Craig's hands to "Haakon's Bedchamber." On the one hand, as we have seen, evidence shows that the ponderously naturalistic "Memling" rendering of the scene found in Poulsen's promptbook (see ills. 2 and 3) was definitely not used in

production, although Craig spent time trying to incorporate it into a preliminary design. Instead, he substituted a very shallow scene, backed by a curtain made of long strips of ribbon and furnished with only the barest essentials. However, the object which he then selected as the focal point of this otherwise austere interior was an immense, canopied four-poster bed decorated in reddish-pink tones! His lighting plan suited the atmosphere: the top projectors were fitted with orange and red gelatines, while smaller lamps were concealed in the bed and even in the cradle itself.[11] "When Skule visits King Haakon in order to negotiate a compromise," observed *Aftenbladet* sarcastically, "he is shown into the royal bedchamber, which more than anything else resembles a Parisian variety star's boudoir." "Much closer to modern French than to ancient Nordic" was the impression which this extraordinary setting made upon Gulman of *Berlingske Tidende* and other critics.

Undoubtedly, however, the most controversial scene design in this generally controversial production was Craig's decor for the death of Bishop Nikolas in the third act. Johannes Poulsen's death scene, imbued with an atmosphere of almost melodramatic foreboding and terror, marked the climax of what was, by virtually all accounts, one of the most notable performances of his long acting career. Poulsen's acting style has been succinctly characterized as "achieving its effect through a monumental simplification, free of all inessential details—like a decorative fresco painting."[12] He played the scheming, treacherous Nikolas "with a great and peculiar intensity, as a very old, toothless man, a half-Jewish ancient, at any rate strongly reminiscent of Shylock" *(Berlingske Tidende)*, and most agreed with *Politiken* that his "octogenarian 'half-man', the libertine cruel in his impotence, will stand out among the gallery of figures he has created as one of his most grotesque—a monumental phantom."

As we might expect, the acting of the death of Nikolas is annotated both in Poulsen's promptbook and (in a more general way) in Craig's own script with meticulous care, in a manner that confirms the critical impression of a performance highlighted by sudden dramatic peripeties. As an actor, Poulsen was generally known for his rather unusual vocal technique. "He adopted his own special stage language," writes the director and designer Svend Gade, who adds that "his own peculiar form of speech lent his performance in serious drama a weightiness and grandeur that none of his contemporaries possessed."[13] "In his death agony his voice is pitiable," wrote one

14. Drawing by Fritz Ahlgrensson of Haakon's banquet scene in 1871. (From *Illustreret Tidende,* January 22, 1871)

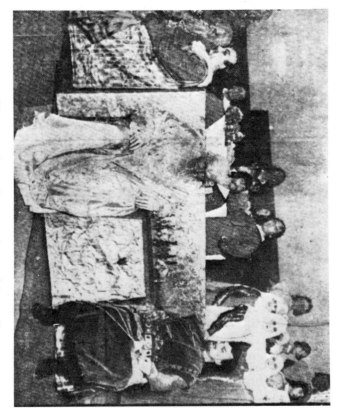

15. Photograph, unfortunately poor in quality,
of Haakon's banquet scene in 1926.
(From *København*, November 15, 1926)

16. Design by Gordon Craig for Bishop Nikolas's death scene (3. 1), "designed after I had made it on the stage." (From Craig, *A Production*)

critic of his Nikolas, "drawling and intoned, but as the urge to do evil once again comes over the dying Bishop, his tone becomes hard and realistic, as far from the churchly tone as is the worst cynic" (*København*). Wind machines were pressed into service to produce an undercurrent of "storm and wind in long, howling blasts" to strengthen the "mystical, religious, nocturnal atmosphere of horror" that Craig and Poulsen endeavored to project into the scene. As the stricken Bishop struggled in the throes of death, the storm cries grew louder and background music was added. The promptbook notes that Nikolas, staggering about the room in mortal terror, "falls down and rolls about on the floor" in his final desperate paroxysm. Then "the light goes out, strange sounds, storm louder."

It was impossible, however, for most observers to reconcile the palpable convulsions and emotional vehemence of Poulsen's death scene with the style of the physical setting provided for it. Treated in Ibsen's stage directions and in the 1899 ground plan as a simple, closed interior which opens into a lighted chapel in the background, the episcopal residence in Oslo was rendered by Craig in a very different fashion. At the very front of his scene he placed an upholstered armchair and an ornate divan with "new bolster." (His preliminary sketches in the Collection Craig testify to his preoccupation with the shape and design of "the bishop's couch," described as "dirty ivory colour, mattress rather thicker, straw coloured.") Behind these pieces of solid furniture, then, one saw the entire depth of the large stage filled with twenty-odd of his gray forms—"high, block-like shapes, some in a greenish light and one of them illuminated with blue."[14]

Poulsen himself seemed pleased enough with the effect, at least in the interview in *Dagens Nyheder* before the opening. "Nothing would have been easier for him, living in Italy, the land of monasteries, to show us a monastery. But he lets the Bishop's death-room consist of an ordinary bare chamber full of long shadows and eeriness." (The Danish director seems to have willingly relinquished his earlier ideas about a medieval chamber painted in the style of Fra Angelico de Fiesole.) The staunchly partisan Vilhelm Saxtorph was also prepared once again to stand in the breach and insist that "the arrangement of the rectangular blocks, which do not directly suggest any specific architecture and of which one is blue and another whitish, contribute in a purely artistic way to the creation of the terrifying atmosphere of the end of the world which is implicit in the Bishop's final expiry."

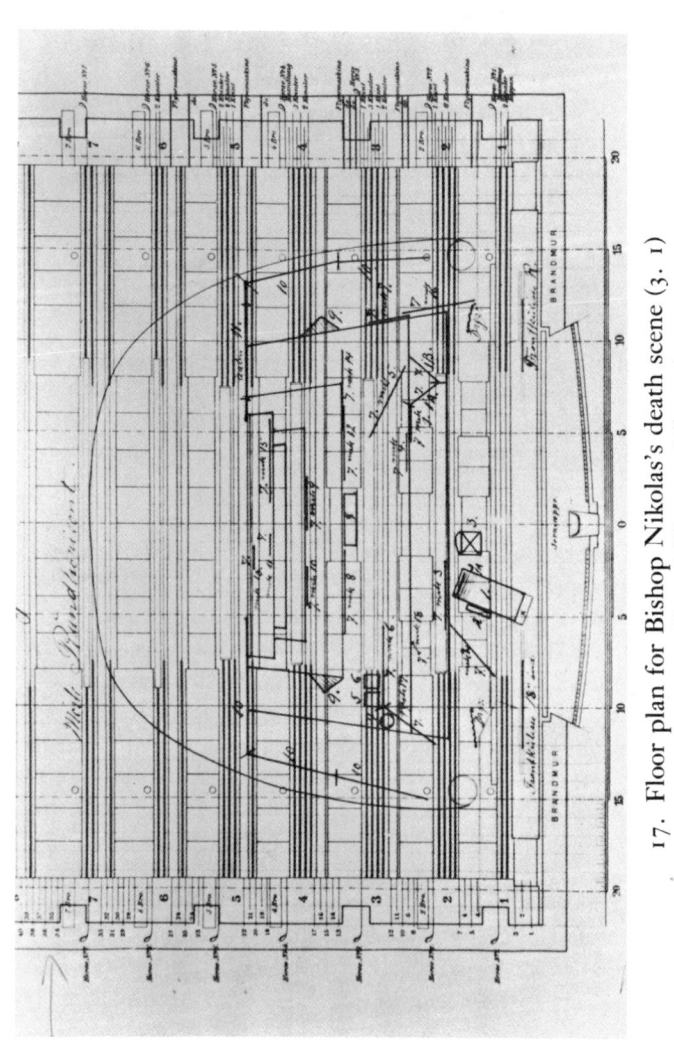

17. Floor plan for Bishop Nikolas's death scene (3. 1) in 1926. (Royal Theatre Library)

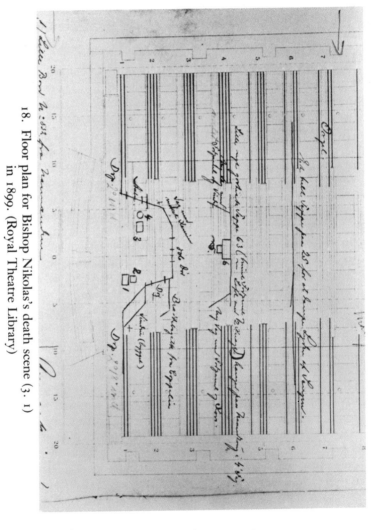

18. Floor plan for Bishop Nikolas's death scene (3. 1)
in 1899. (Royal Theatre Library)

Such sentiments found no sympathy among the other critics, however, who were universally and outspokenly unimpressed. "The Bishop's room, resembling a warehouse cellar in the dockyards, filled with packing cases, robbed [Johannes Poulsen's performance] of all its mystique, in spite of a violet spotlight on one of the packing cases," declared *København*. "Bishop Nikolas dies on a sofa that has been moved out into the open air—in Oslo!" exclaimed Cavling in *Politiken*. "The Bishop's moving death scene was acted in something resembling a churchyard, in which he breathes his last on a divan," grumbled *Aftenbladet*. "The strange blocks among which the Bishop dies were," Valdemar Vedel stated categorically in *Dagens Nyheder*, among the most unfortunate elements in the production. Of the multiple design projects for this scene which Craig publishes and describes in *A Production*, the one he identifies as having been used in Copenhagen (consisting of "eight small screens rising one behind the other, as can be seen, and a pallet bed") is probably the most evocative and the most "Craigish" sketch in the entire portfolio (ills. 16, 17, and 18). Nevertheless, however interesting in theory, its relationship to actual practice is tenuous—Craig notes that it was "designed after I had made it on the stage"—and any evaluation of its effectiveness in the theatre must needs be developed in the rather unflattering light of the foregoing critical responses and the startlingly prosaic photograph of the scene that appeared in *Politiken* (ill. 19).

A much closer bond between the conception of the artist and its realization on the stage seems to have been forged in Craig's rendering of the two exterior scenes with which *The Pretenders* concludes. In the first of these (5. 2), Bishop Nikolas appears as a ghost from hell to tempt and taunt the frightened Skule in mocking, ironic verse.[15] While a naturalistically inclined critic like Archer would inevitably regard this ghost scene as "a great and flagrant blemish . . . a sheer excrescence on the play," Craig would, just as inevitably, welcome the apparition as a splendid opportunity, a visualized symbol of the mysterious inner forces at work in the drama. "The fact of their presence precludes a realistic treatment of the tragedies in which they appear," he writes of the ghosts in Shakespeare's plays. "These spirits are the key to which, as in music, every note of the composition must be harmonized; they are integral, not extraneous parts of the drama."[16]

The setting in which the spectre appears—a misty, moonlit pinewood on the hills above Nidaros—was treated as simply by Craig as it

19. Photograph of Bishop Nikolas's death scene (3. 1)
in 1926. (From *Politiken*, November 15, 1926)

had been in Fru Heiberg's production fifty-five years earlier: in 1871,
the scenery had consisted solely of "a wild, deserted view (new), stage
right a rock"; on Craig's stage one saw only a large, irregularly shaped
set piece suggesting a snowbank and a large, luminous back curtain
that "rose into the air like the wall of a cliff or a group of tree-
trunks."[17] Ibsen's stage directions indicate that "the background can
be seen only indistinctly and sometimes not at all"; accordingly, as the
procession with Haakon's wife and child passes while Skule and his
companions conceal themselves, Poulsen's promptbook notes that a
scrim, or "fog curtain," descends and "snow [another of Nielsen's
projection effects] begins to fall more and more thickly." Later, when
Skule has been left alone with the mysterious monk—none other than
the infernal spirit of Bishop Nikolas—"the fog curtain is raised again
to a man's height. The snow decreases."

The ground plan (ill. 20) reveals that not one of the preliminary
studies for the ghost scene reproduced by Craig in *A Production* was
actually used directly; however, the drawing shown in illustration 21
evokes a vivid sense of the atmosphere which Craig sought to create
on the stage. The most interesting feature of this particular sketch is,
however, its source of inspiration. Shortly after his arrival in

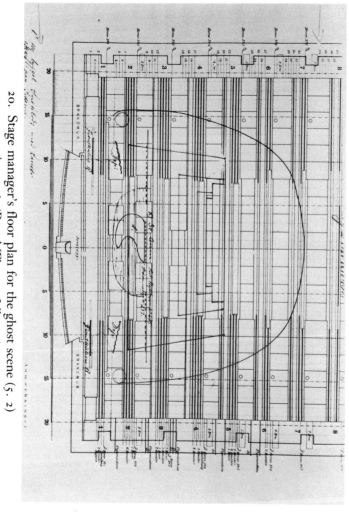

20. Stage manager's floor plan for the ghost scene (5. 2)
in 1926. (Royal Theatre Library)

21. Preliminary design project by Gordon Craig
for the ghost scene.
(From Craig, *A Production*)

Copenhagen, Craig attended Johannes Poulsen's colorful and historically authentic production of the popular Viggo Cavling ballet, *Tycho Brahes Drøm* [The dream of Tycho Brahe], at the Royal Theatre, starring Ulla Poulsen as the peasant girl with whom the great sixteenth-century astronomer (a pantomimic role, played by Poulsen himself) falls in love.[18] After the performance he hastened to write to his new collaborator.

9 Oct. 1926

Dear Johannes Poulsen.

Are you tired of hearing your praises from people? Anyhow tolerate it from a brother artist. I thought the setting & mise en scene of the Ballet *was beautifull* [sic]. You will make a *great* effect with your [arrow pointing to a sketch he had made on the page] and I have the determination to discover at least *one little* touch to add to it so I may be with you all even in that.[19]

The drawing contained in Craig's letter, depicting his impression of Poulsen as Brahe, standing beside the great tower of his famous observatory, and framed against the star-filled night sky, corresponds in detail both to the finished sketch he finally published and to a pencil drawing of the ghost walk in *The Pretenders* found in the Poulsen promptbook (see ill. 22). Clearly, however, anyone who recalls the *Study for Movement* which Craig sketched around 1906 and later published in *Towards a New Theatre*, depicting a man standing beside a towering tree trunk and struggling against the wind and snow, will recognize yet another instance of the marked relationship between Craig's work for *The Pretenders* and his experiments twenty years earlier.

"Shades—spirits seem to me to be more beautiful, and filled with more vitality than men and women," Craig liked to insist,[20] and this avowed preoccupation with the supernatural is illustrated by the variety of different preliminary projects and studies for the ghost scene which he included in *A Production*. One of his most atmospheric ghost projects, seen in illustrations 23 and 24, also reminds us that he rarely wasted a good idea. The original for this particular drawing, with its windswept rendering of the eerie apparition, is to be found on his copy of an invitation to the gala opening-night party, which he returned to the Poulsens with his note of acceptance, suitably illustrated!

In the convent yard at Elgesæter, where Skule and his ruthless son Peter meet their deaths at the hands of the outraged citizens of

22. Page from Johannes Poulsen's promptbook,
showing a drawing of the ghost walk.
(Royal Theatre Library)

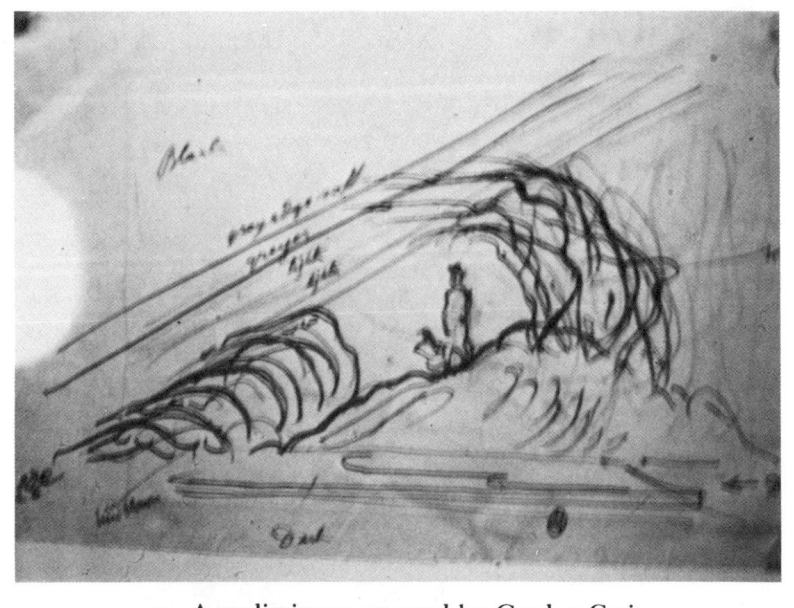

23. A preliminary proposal by Gordon Craig
for transferring his idea of the ghost scene
to the stage. (Bibliothèque Nationale, Paris)

Nidaros who had been forced by them to rebel against Haakon, *The Pretenders* reaches its violent and moving climax. The fascinating design which Craig created for this final scene (ills. 25 and 26) brings us full circle, invoking as it does a direct and basic contrast with the very first illustration shown, P. F. Wergmann's design for Ibsen's own production of the play in 1864. Wergmann's admirably clear pictorialization of Ibsen's stage directions epitomizes a tradition of historical illusionism which was still vigorous when Lehmann revived the play at the Royal Theatre thirty-five years later. The ground plan for the 1899 production (see ills. 27 and 28, which provide a visual comparison between the 1926 and 1899 floor plans) delineates an open playing area bordered on the right by "four pieces of new church" with a practicable porch and door, on the left by similarly painted flats representing low convent buildings, and at the back by "two pieces of new wall" and a sturdy gate ("key in the lock," adds the careful stage manager). Hence, apart from the "modern" deference to asymmetry evident in the catercorner position of the church and the oblique line of the rear wall, this ground plan shares with the Werg-

mann design the same fundamental attitude toward the problem of re-creating on stage the specific place where the historical Skule met his fate.

Diametrically opposed to this attitude, Craig (if one may be permitted to plagiarize Appia for a moment) was concerned not with the depiction of a *place*—that is, the illusion of a courtyard with characters in it—but with the living presence of *characters in an atmosphere*, of Skule trapped both physically within the sanctuary of the convent yard and psychologically within his own moral dilemma. Viewed in this way, the dark, dominant image at the center of Craig's stage—the two strangely shaped gates, one behind the other, with a third visible in the background, the twisting network of low picket fences that crisscross the permanent structure of platforms almost like the barbed wire on a First World War battlefield—seems to become an impressionistic projection of Skule's inner struggle.

In this case, Craig's thinking seems at first to have followed a much less symbolic and more representational path. His papers in the

24. Gordon Craig's finished design for the version of the ghost scene shown in illustration 23. (From Craig, *A Production*)

71

**25.** Design by Gordon Craig for
the last scene of *The Pretenders.*
(From Craig, *A Production*)

26. Details from Johannes Poulsen's promptbook for the
last scene of *The Pretenders*. Part of the text refers
to the conclusion of the ghost scene preceding act
5, scene 3. "Blast of wind and laughter. His laughter
is heard in the dark. Skule collapses in the snow
[deletion]." Note the deletion of "Moonlight—clear—
stars" from the description of the final scene.
(Royal Theatre Library)

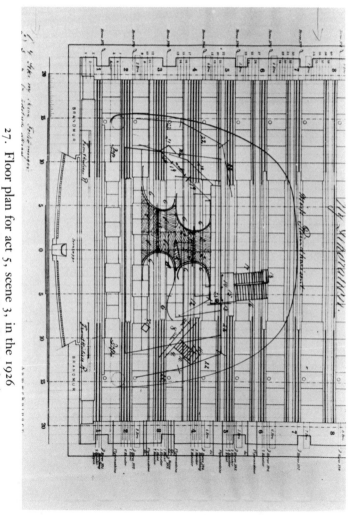

27. Floor plan for act 5, scene 3, in the 1926
production, corresponding in detail to Craig's design.
(Royal Theatre Library)

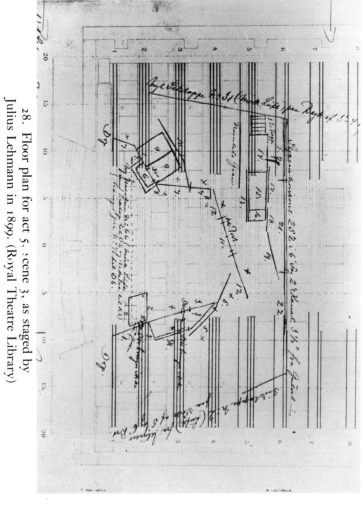

28. Floor plan for act 5, scene 3, as staged by Julius Lehmann in 1899. (Royal Theatre Library)

Collection Craig include a much more realistic conception of a towering iron gate and a shadowy figure in the moonlight, executed both as a small colored drawing in his copy of the text—marked "Moonlight not used. Done before getting to Copenhagen"—and as a full-scale scene design. Another preliminary sketch of the gate is annotated, "(Realistic or not as needed) A piece on runners—consisting of steps up to a gateway & a green (or grey) slope down on the other side." Yet another note in his workbook reads, "Perhaps something 1904 is suitable for the end." This latter idea assumes its proper context when we remember that the first rough sketch of "The Gates" for *The Pretenders* is actually to be found in Craig's interleaved text for *The Vikings of Helgeland*, which he staged in London in 1903.[21]

In Craig's scene as we now know it, everything else in the stage picture is subordinated to the controlling image of the twisting, constrictive fence. Ibsen's "chapel with lighted windows"—necessary because Skule's women must seek refuge within it—is now little more than a suggestion, placed well below and behind the main platform. Of the low convent buildings over which the savage Peter climbs to gain access to the courtyard, only the merest indication of a roof and cloisters remains. Even the "clear moonlit night" indicated by the stage directions (and transcribed and subsequently crossed out on the promptbook page seen in ill. 26) has been abandoned in favor of a sky of brilliant green, broken only by two thin, horizontal stripes of clear light, two parallel and finely drawn cloud lines. ("May I again suggest *straight white lines* in sky, not curved ones," remarks a beleaguered Craig in his dress-rehearsal notes.) The designer's muted symbolism is evocative, not restrictive: every element of his carefully integrated composition—line and color, lighting effects and groupings—is designed to reveal the play, to present a visual pattern that will enable the spectator to respond emotionally to Skule's struggle to attain his realization that "there are men created to live and men created to die."

In Craig's interpretation it was essential, moreover, that nothing melodramatic or "theatrical" should attach itself to Skule's final moments of self-recognition. "Skule ordinary and *at ease* when he goes to die," reads a characteristic remark scrawled by Craig on a large, loose sheet of paper: "Really at ease—because *no more uneasy*." As Skule takes his leave of wife, daughter, and sister in this scene, his attitude must, insists Craig in his interleaved text, remain entirely joyful and proud: "The gaiety of nobility doubting. Gay, please—but really strong & gay & all the house will be howling." As Sigrid, his sister,

announces exultantly that "all the bells of Nidaros are ringing," Skule's reply ("They are ringing a King to his grave") must make him appear, in Craig's view, neither "pathetic" nor "a tragedy king" but instead "still gay & proud." Even as he turns to address the angry mob ("I come. The church robber will come too"), Craig's image of Skule must remain "all very athletic and trim," still "gay—clear—laughing quietly" in his delivery. ("Adam Poulsen tried hard," reads a tersely worded note of disappointment, added later by Craig.) In visual terms, Skule's final heroic decision to sacrifice his life to prevent further bloodshed transforms the oppressive, cagelike gates of Craig's scene into portals, through which he passes, for the first time, on to "the path that God has pointed out" for him: "Join in prayer; sing a message to the Lord and tell him that Skule Baardsson comes home, a penitent, from his lawless journey upon earth."

Unfortunately, the absence of any truly consistent style or vision in most of the foregoing scenes left the critics less disposed to respond to symbolic simplification at this point in the production. "Here," complained one exponent of literal-mindedness, "we find, among other things, some gates so low that anyone could stride over them. Nevertheless, the citizens hammer in despair against the match-wood and control their wild passions until the Earl has converted himself into a better and repentant person" *(Aftenbladet)*. While other observers were inclined to describe the picket fence scene as "Russian" or even "Japanese" in style, few were convinced that Craig had responded effectively to the specifically Nordic tone and atmosphere of Ibsen's drama. "One can also make the point," remarked Valdemar Vedel in even more general terms, "that all such attempts at simplification will invariably produce, at the outset at least, the opposite effect from what is intended, in that the new way will always distract and seem much more obtrusive than that of neutral custom."

In fairness both to Craig and to his critics, meanwhile, it must be admitted that the acting performances of the two principal characters in this scene appear to have conspired to obscure the interpretative concept underlying it. Adam Poulsen, appearing, on the occasion of his silver jubilee, as a special guest artist on the Royal Theatre stage, was inevitably a commanding and heroic Skule throughout, sincere and immensely imposing with his clear, sonorous delivery, without any trace of the Macbeth that must lurk within the character if his final "conversion" is to make much sense in the theatre. Poulsen's "Norwegian Hamlet," though heavily made up with mephistophe-

lean eyebrows and a demonic red wig and beard, nonetheless re-mained an unthreatening and shadowless figure. "The deeply tragic side of Skule, the smouldering coals that scorch but never quite dare to burst into flame, remained beyond his power," wrote the reviewer for *København*. "All the darkness in Skule was made light by the tones of his lyrical voice, it disappeared, was gone."

As his rival, the Haakon of Eyvind Johan-Svendsen presented an equally unexpected contrast—a dark, short, robust figure ("a Musso-lini, convinced of his mission, who goes fearlessly forward to his goal," one critic was even led to remark) who possessed none of the physical features of Ibsen's blond Nordic hero, though he certainly seems to have embodied Craig's own antiromantic view of the charac-ter. In this Haakon, luminous confidence seemed continually tinged by shadow. "No star shines above his head," commented *Dagens Nyheder*, "and his kingly thought cast neither resonance over his gruff voice nor light over his inelegant figure." One cannot help but specu-late that, if the casting of these two roles had been reversed, Craig's interpretation of the final scene and the darker implications of his symbolic decor might have carried greater force and conviction in performance.

The slaying of Skule by the mob outside the convent gates during the closing moments of *The Pretenders* represents a distinct and en-grossing problem in the production history of the play. In its first Royal Theatre production in 1871, Skule and Peter were killed outside the gate, amidst "wild noise"; Fru Heiberg was convinced, however, that to leave Skule's corpse stretched outside on the threshold, as the stage directions indicate, while the last lines are spoken about him would be to risk an anticlimax or even laughter, and accordingly the body was borne onstage by the Earl's men before the final curtain fell. Characteristically, she also persuaded Ibsen to end his play by assigning Sigrid's line about her brother's "lawless jour-ney upon earth" to the victorious Haakon, thereby eliminating the problematic reference to Skule as "God's stepchild on earth"—for in Fru Heiberg's world, if not in Ibsen's, no merciful and all-loving God could possibly have stepchildren on his green earth.[22] The revival in 1899 solved the "problem" of the recumbent Skule in a rather diffe-rent fashion: after Haakon has stepped across the body of his slain rival in order to gain access to the courtyard, Lehmann's promptbook tersely notes that "the bodies are carried off."[23] Ibsen's closing speech about Skule was retained intact, but after Haakon had delivered it,

the promptbook adds that "the crowd comes in and shouts, Hail!"

Craig's scene design, with its series of cagelike gates, opened up an entirely new range of possibilities for staging this concluding sequence. The overriding atmosphere of emotional turmoil and mob violence that Poulsen obviously sought to generate in this scene is evident even in the tone of his detailed promptbook notes. As the Skule of this production opened the first of the gates to face the mob—characterized by one observer as "the wolves, the murderers, a disordered huddle of people, a chaos of savage instincts"—he "releases [Peter's] hand, goes out through the first gate, and says to the wild beasts, '—but do not cut his face'—they answer him with fierce, threatening growls. Skule now turns and calls the boy, he comes up to him and closes first gate."

An instant later, amid general shouts from the mob to "Strike where you can," the victims "are surrounded and crushed. Short fight, wild noise." As Skule and Peter are slaughtered in the area between the two gates, five men were instructed to leap over the fence and crouch in front of the first gate, presumably in order to conceal the disposal of the corpses. After the two had fallen, the atmosphere of violence and cruelty was further heightened by means of a sudden, effective silence: "all heads bowed and looking down at them."

With the arrival of Haakon and his followers, the audience was treated to one further shock. As Dagfinn the Peasant enters ("This way, King Haakon!"), "he goes through second gate and through first gate—Skule is seen hanging [on a hook] on the door, the boy lying below him." When the King demurs briefly ("His body blocks my way"), a helpful citizen "cuts Skule down to please Haakon" and the corpse "falls down over the edge of the step" (though this last, almost Artaudian touch receives a large red query in the promptbook). Understandably horrified by this display of Nidarosian blood-lust, Haakon and his sixteen Birkebeiners pause where they are. "The entire crowd remains behind the body, all look at Skule's corpse and look toward Haakon."

The indecisiveness passes and on Ibsen's cue ("In God's name, then!") the conqueror steps over the body—but he remains "deeply moved and actually afraid: he turns again and goes up to the corpse." Dagfinn, the alert and honest counselor, senses trouble and speaks ("At last you can begin your royal task") with the specific objective of calming his uneasy sovereign. "Dagfinn's voice (& very quiet & few movements) is like that of a nurse with a child," writes Craig in his

79

own copy of the text. Presumably in order to underscore this character's bluff and skeptical nature, a curiously embellished last line was
also concocted for him: "A mystery? What sort of mystery would that
be? Why, the doomed beast died frightened and silent."

Haakon's reply, his brief closing apostrophe to "God's stepchild,"
was given every theatrical advantage: Dagfinn was sent upstage to
join the impressive tableau in the background; the bells of Nidaros
had ceased a beat earlier, and "strong singing" was now heard as
Haakon spoke. As he finished, he turned halfway round to look down
once more at the sprawled corpse of his defeated opponent—and then
he drew "a deep, deep breath" which he slowly exhaled. (Behind
Poulsen's direction at this point lies the explanatory interpretative
note made by Craig in his own copy: "His first doubt is born now.
Begins one immensely puzzled sigh—for he is a man of purpose—he
sometimes suspects he is the honest fool he is—perhaps he has
another look at Skule.") On this long, portentous sigh by Haakon,
Craig's cartographic Gobelin curtain was rung down for the last time.

## CHAPTER SIX

## THE PROBLEM OF

## COSTUME STYLE

The minor character of Dagfinn the Peasant, portrayed with great effectiveness in the 1926 production of *The Pretenders* by Valdemar Møller, provides a useful transition to the crucial subject of costume style as it relates to Gordon Craig's overall scenic conception (see ill. 29). It must come as a surprise to anyone who peruses *A Production* for the first time that Dagfinn is, in fact, the *only* identifiable character for whom Craig has included a costume sketch. He offers no indication whatsoever of the style of costuming worn by the major characters.

The "three costume sketches derived from ancient manuscripts" which Craig includes are obviously preliminary studies having no demonstrable connection to what was actually done in practice; a colorful design for a peasant boy's costume ("3 cloaks each—carrying other cloaks . . . so as not to wave the arms") seems a pleasant reprise of his Old Gobbo in the *Merchant of Venice* series (1909), without much apparent relationship to the atmosphere of Ibsen's play; and his splendidly grotesque sketch of the ghost ("The fleshless arm, I took it, might swing in the wind, lifelessly") is surely intended to be taken with a grain of salt (see ill. 30). However, the absence of any more concrete sketches for specific costumes can certainly not be taken as evidence of indifference to this side of the production, for we know that Craig was adamant about the significant place of costuming in the general design of a play. The color, cut, texture, and flow of a

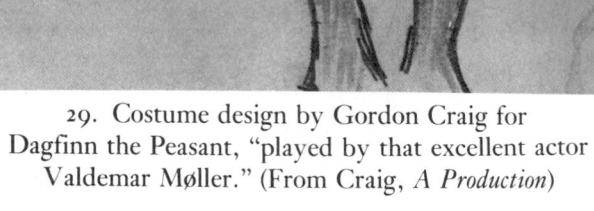

29. Costume design by Gordon Craig for
Dagfinn the Peasant, "played by that excellent actor
Valdemar Møller." (From Craig, *A Production*)

30. Sketch by Gordon Craig of Bishop Nikolas's ghost. "The fleshless arm, I took it, might swing in the wind, lifelessly." (From Craig, *A Production*)

garment were all meant to be integrated into the conception of scene and movement which he evolved for a given work. Nor does the blithe assumption that Craig had no hand in the actual designing of new costumes for *The Pretenders* withstand critical scrutiny.

Although documentary sources pertaining to the costuming of this production are lacking in the Royal Theatre archives, significant evidence is to be found in the Bibliothèque Nationale which sheds new light on Craig's work in this regard. Here, among much else, is to be found the Royal Theatre's official costume list (in Danish!) for the 1926 production—evidently carried away by Craig when he left Copenhagen—as well as a typed transcript, annotated with penciled translations, of the costume and properties list for the first production of the play at the Royal Theatre in 1871.

For this first performance of the work, staged by Johanne Luise Heiberg, a wardrobe of new costumes was naturally required to accommodate the colorful gallery of warriors, monks, medieval burghers, and noblemen with which Ibsen had populated his romantic saga drama. The costuming and movement of the actor on the romantic stage contributed in large measure to its predominantly pictorial character. Hence the primary aim of stage costuming in a production such as this was not to preserve strict historical verisimilitude above all else, but rather to add an evocative and picturesque flavor, a splash of color and a wealth of rich materials to the depiction of history and the past.

Fortunately for our purposes, the costume designs for the Fru Heiberg production have survived in the Royal Theatre Library, and these offer a vivid impression of general stylistic principles. The pseudohistorical costumes worn by Haakon, Skule, and Peter in 1871, seen in illustrations 31 and 32, have a fundamentally similar outline—belted, knee-length tunics, cowls and ornate berets (replaced in Peter's case by armor), sword, hose, and ankle shoes—and they reflect, not unexpectedly, the influence of historical paintings and relevant engravings. Haakon's royal attire, heavily trimmed with gold and furs and ornamented with the fashionable loose-hanging sleeves of the period, is a particularly good illustration of the tendency toward a richer and more elaborate style of costuming that grew as the century progressed.[1]

As Bishop Nikolas, Emil Poulsen is seen in this series of costume designs dressed in the full ecclesiastical regalia of his vocation. A rather different but by no means less opulent version of the Bishop's

31. Three costume designs for the 1871 production
of *The Pretenders. Left to right:* a monk, Earl Skule
("N.B. hood on collar"), and Haakon ("grey tights").
(Royal Theatre Library)

costuming is given in a hand-colored sketch (see ill. 33) drawn by Fritz
Ahlgrensson, which the late Robert Neiiendam brought to light some
years ago. (In Emil Poulsen's own day, it would seem that neither of
these two drawings of him in the role were known to exist. At least, as
the fame of his performance as Nikolas spread gradually through
Europe, Josef Lewinsky, who was preparing to act the role in 1891 at
the Burgtheater in Vienna, asked to see a picture of his Danish
colleague in the part—only to be told that none was to be found.)[2]

By 1926, of course, radical changes in attitude and in style had
already taken place. It required no Gordon Craig to repeat the familiar axiom that actual reality can never be reproduced on the stage,
and, this being so, any attempt to represent historical "authenticity"
in the theatre is invariably a subtle lie. (Does anyone really believe
that nineteenth-century theatre artists like Charles Kean and Johanne
Luise Heiberg were so naive that they failed to recognize that truism?)

32. Three costume designs for the 1871 production
of *The Pretenders*. *Left to right:* Master Sigard,
Peter ("second costume"), and Bishop Nikolas.
(Royal Theatre Library)

Craig himself had long since proclaimed the need for a new, "imaginative" style of costuming ("a barbaric costume for a sly man which has nothing about it which can be said to be historical and yet is both sly and barbaric") and had consequently urged the abandonment of "the costume books" as a guide.

Remain clear and fresh. If you study how to draw a figure, how to put on it a jacket, coverings for the legs, covering for the head, and try to vary these coverings in all kinds of interesting, amusing, or beautiful ways, you will get much further than if you feast your eyes and confound your brain with Racinet, Planchet [that is, presumably, James Robinson Planché], Hottenroth, and the others. . . . Better than these that I have mentioned is Viollet le Duc. He has much love for truths which underlie costume, and is very faithful in his attitude; but even his is more a book for the historical novelist, and one has yet to be written about imaginative costume.[3]

In Copenhagen, one might expect that Craig would put such pronouncements into practice. In a preperformance interview, Johannes Poulsen repeated with approval the advice he had received from Craig about costuming.

Do not become too obsessed with the period picture. Do not encase the modern spirits Ibsen has created in armor from the thirteenth century. It is not a question of giving the spectators a lesson in history. Do not worry about correctness. That which is at stake is to get the audience to relive the visions which the playwright had while turning the play over in his mind. If we can get them to see his visions, our objective is achieved.[4]

In Craig's work at its best, meanwhile, this repudiation of historical "correctness" and adherence to "the period picture" in costuming and scenery was counterbalanced by a highly developed awareness of the traditions and conventions of the past. "To judge from his work he is not so much a revolutionary as a reformer," wrote one critic of the Moscow *Hamlet*, for example. "Far from being an enemy to theatrical tradition, he seems to realize better than any one how much valuable material for his art lies buried in that limbo of things forgotten."[5] In describing the famous experiments with marionettes, masks, and optical mixtures, Edward Craig places a similar emphasis on his father's belief that all these projects "meant that the past must be studied too, for he had written 'Never copy the old but *never forget the old*—for there is always some good to be found in it.' "[6] However, although the immense historical resources and venerable traditions of the Royal Theatre would seem to have provided an ideal opportunity to apply this approach, Craig appears to have encountered great difficulty in achieving a consistent style of costuming compatible with Ibsen's vision and with his own nonrepresentational scenography for *The Pretenders*.

As already mentioned, Craig was assisted in his labors by Svend Johansen, later to become one of the Scandinavian theatre's foremost modern designers, who had been assigned by the Royal Theatre to help in the task of creating new costumes for this production. Johansen, a professional to the fingertips, unfortunately soon found himself out of patience with Craig's methods, and their relationship ended in disagreement. "He had heaps of ideas and he himself thought they were all equally splendid, while I was of the presumptuous opinion that ninety percent should be thrown out simply because they were

33. Sketch by Fritz Ahlgrensson of Emil Poulsen in the role of Bishop Nikolas, 1871. (Danish Theatre Museum)

dilettantish," Johansen remarks tartly in his memoirs, adding that the production ended as "a strange conglomerate, in a style that may be best described as Manchurian-cubist-quattrocento-Italian Renaissance in midnight sunshine."[7]

The Danish designer recalls that his chief task was to provide costumes for Haakon's sixteen Birkebeiners. "So far as I understood, they were some northern Norwegian peasant rebels in skins and birchbark, but heaven help us, what Birkebeiners we managed to patch together. I was set to copying costumes out of the works of Viollet le Duc, and the Birch-legs turned out as something fantastic to behold, in full-length velvet capes and with thirteen-foot tournament lances in their hands, roughly as in Paolo Uccello's battle pictures." Disregarding Johansen's obvious sarcasm, his recollection of copying out costumes from le Duc at Craig's behest nonetheless sheds rather startling light on the discrepancy that sometimes prevailed between Craig's professed theories and his practice.

During their brief and uneasy collaboration, poor Craig must surely have felt ill at ease under the contemptuous scrutiny of his brilliant but rebellious assistant, who "to make things really complicated and scientific" borrowed from the noted Danish sculptor Einar Utzon-Frank a lovely statuette "which we used as a kind of dressmaker's model. Frank had treated it with piss and acid to give it patina," the unrepentant Johansen continues, "and when Gordon Craig saw it, he asked me if it was an antique! Never mind, we all can make mistakes—I have even seen rich Americans in Florence who thought that Donatello was a kind of stone."[8] Inevitably, this rumbustious collaborator found himself dismissed as "an impossible idiot," and his name is nowhere to be found in Craig's sumptuous portfolio, *A Production*.

Had the story ended here, it would be an entertaining but scarcely significant anecdote. It has, however, an interesting sequel. Among the most remarkable of all the sources and documents related to this production and preserved in the archives of the Royal Theatre is a collection of twenty-six colored designs and preliminary pencil sketches for costumes in *The Pretenders*, executed by Svend Johansen. Johansen, already firmly established as one of the most exciting and revolutionary modernist painters in Scandinavia, was at this point on the threshold of his long and successful career as a stage designer. His collection of sketches for *The Pretenders*, which includes not only designs for many of the supernumeraries but also finished costume

34. Costume sketches by Svend Johansen for
*The Pretenders.*
*Left to right:* a monk and King Haakon.
(Royal Theatre Library)

concepts for most of the principal characters in the play, affords a sparkling foretaste of the distinctive theatrical style that quickly became his trademark: "Like Cézanne and the cubists, who reshaped figures in order to fit them into a pictorial composition, Svend Johansen deforms his figures expressionistically, in order to express and to underscore—in burlesque fashion—that which he finds characteristic about them."[9]

Hence, the figure of the young monk in illustration 34, wearing a light grey robe *painted* with silver accents, is designed by Johansen to make a witty stylistic comment on the traditional conception of this character in, for instance, the nineteenth-century production of the play by Fru Heiberg (cf. ill. 31). In the same pair of illustrations, Eyvind Johan-Svendsen's richly ornamental King Haakon, decked out in a black velvet tunic elaborately decorated with gold and green stones, presents an expressionistically barbaric reinterpretation of the

conventional style of historical attire worn by his counterpart, J. L. Nyrop, in 1871. In a somewhat similar vein, Johansen's conception of Master Sigard (ill. 35), the sedate physician who attends the dying Bishop Nikolas, appears to transpose the older costume for this part (ill. 32) into a new and subtly ironic key.

For Skule's fanatical son Peter, the designer conceived a costume (ill. 36) that marks an even more striking departure from the rather naive quality of the older design, seen in illustration 32. Consisting of a dark, rakishly cut velvet tunic with "metal sleeves," decorated with silver ornaments and low-slung sword belt and matched by fashionably long-nosed velvet shoes, it conveys, to a modern spectator, a much sharper sense of Peter's inherent arrogance and cruelty. For Adam Poulsen's Skule, Johansen naturally sketched a variety of

35. Costume sketches by Svend Johansen for
*The Pretenders.*
*Left to right:* Master Sigard and Earl Skule.
(Royal Theatre Library)

36. Costume sketch by Svend Johansen of
Peter "as Skule's son" in *The Pretenders*.
(Royal Theatre Library)

37. Photograph of Adam Poulsen in the
role of Skule. (Bibliothèque Nationale, Paris)

costume projects, each of which skillfully combines the flavor of the period with what might be called oblique physical suggestions of the character's inner nature—that is, a note of ambitiousness in the lavish fur trim and fastidiously elongated sleeves of his regal dress, a hint of the character's fundamental vacillation and self-doubt in the abstract pattern of broad, undulating stripes imposed across the sleeves and the entire body of his battle attire. (The latter design, seen in illustration 35, bears the pencil notation, "The stripes wavy and in *one* direction.")

The chief critical question which arises, of course, is twofold: To which extent were these costume designs by Svend Johansen actually made use of in the performance, and what relationship do they then have to Craig's own work in this area? There seems to have been a general tendency among those who are aware of the existence of Johansen's collection of drawings for *The Pretenders* to assume that none of them ever was actually utilized in practice. However, a good deal of evidence exists to contradict this assumption. Alone the incongruous fact that many of them are inscribed with notes and directions almost surely intended for the guidance of those engaged in the manufacture of the completed costumes arrests our attention.

Perhaps the most significant piece of evidence in this respect is the official costume list itself, which Craig—for reasons known only to himself—evidently took with him when he departed. This document, which is stamped by the Royal Theatre stage manager's office and is dated October 25, 1926, is signed by none other than Johansen himself, who provides here a scene-by-scene inventory of costumes needed for the supernumeraries, dividing them into those already in stock and those now "being manufactured." Four days after the date on this costume list, Johansen was interviewed in *Nationaltidende*, where he describes his collaboration with the "curious" Gordon Craig (including a less robust reference to their model work on Utzon-Frank's patinaed statuette!) and replies unequivocally that he is indeed "making the costumes" for the production.

Among Craig's own papers in the Bibliothèque Nationale are numerous items—including memoranda in Danish and costume details and sketches obviously drawn by Johansen himself—that emphasize the (subsequently obliterated) contribution of the Danish designer to this aspect of the production. Of particular interest is a fragmentary slip of paper containing a note in Craig's hand initially dated November 4, asking Johansen to show Craig costumes for

Skule, Hakon, Bishop, Margaret [sic], Sigrid, Mrs. Skule, and Inger [sic], with a further notation by Craig that this was not done until November 10. Even by November 10, it would seem, Johansen never did manage (or bother) to show these finished costumes to his English colleague, and, in the critical notes made by Craig at the dress rehearsal two days later, elaborate care seems to have been taken to avoid any mention of Johansen's name. "As I see it all the costumes of Scene 1 wrong colours, because chosen without showing to any one and me." There is, in the final analysis, no direct evidence to indicate that the majority of Johansen's costume designs for the principal characters were ever realized in practice. Nonetheless, several of the published newspaper photographs reveal clearly enough a style of costuming that is unquestionably a reflection of—and may actually have found its inspiration in—the approach to line, texture, and historical period which Johansen's drawings adopt. Surely the battle dress worn by Adam Poulsen's heroic and manly Skule, seen in the photograph reproduced in illustration 37, bears an unmistakable relationship to the style of costume envisioned for his belligerent son Peter in Johansen's series of designs (ill. 36).

The second half of the problem—the actual relationship between Johansen's work and Craig's contribution—is even more fraught with difficulties. Craig himself is deliberately and tantalizingly evasive about the real sources of origin of the various costumes used in *The Pretenders*. " 'A few new costumes have been specially made.' I feel that this should be announced," he comments at one point in his rehearsal memoranda. But to which new costumes (as distinct from those borrowed from stock) does he refer? And by whom were they made?

There is no doubt whatsoever that the costume design for Dagfinn the Peasant which Craig reproduces in *A Production* (see ill. 29) represents a fully accurate rendering of the actual costume that was ultimately made for and worn by this character in the performance. It is most disconcerting, however, to discover among Svend Johansen's designs yet another finished sketch of the rotund Valdemar Møller as Dagfinn (ill. 38), clad in a graphically barbaric peasant's dress of leather and skins that corresponds in every principal detail (except for the angle from which the figure in drawn) to Craig's published design.

The problem is not made simpler by the fact that the Dagfinn design found in the Bibliothèque Nationale is itself a copy (on which the character's name is misspelled), made by Craig and identified as

38. Costume design for Dagfinn the Peasant
in *The Pretenders*. (Royal Theatre Library)

follows: "The finished drawing made from this sketch and reproduced in *A Production* (Plate XXXI) is in the possession of Vald. Møller, who played Dagfinn." Clearly, while Craig refrains steadfastly from any mention of his uneasy collaboration with Svend Johansen, his published version of this particular costume design (with its unexplained use of the Danish word *flip*—that is, "collar") must presumably be one of three things: either an unacknowledged copy of an earlier design by Johansen (a rather distasteful possibility to contemplate), or the original concept from which the Johansen sketch (if it *is* his and not Craig's) is itself surreptitiously copied (a somewhat unlikely possibility, in view of the Danish artist's outspoken lack of confidence in Craig's abilities), or, finally, the original concept, of which both the copy in the Collection Craig *and* the variant now found in the Royal Theatre Library are preliminary versions drawn, at various times, by Craig himself (the hypothesis which the present authors prefer to adopt). If one looks back to the early design for Haakon's wedding banquet which Craig completed in Genoa (ill. 11), it is clear enough that, already at this point, it is the same general concept that he uses in depicting Dagfinn, seated between Paul Flida and Gregorius Jonsson in the lower left-hand corner of the picture.

On the other hand, there are several instances in which Johansen's spirit and technique seem to suffuse costume drawings to which Craig puts his own name. For example, one of the three unidentified figures "derived from ancient manuscripts" and reproduced in plate XXX of *A Production* seems to be a distinct but less ironic echo of Johansen's design for Master Sigard, the physician to Bishop Nikolas. A much more striking case is exemplified by a drawing in the Bibliothèque Nationale which Craig has initialled but which he chose *not* to reproduce (see ill. 39)—a rather tipsy-looking representative of Skule's knights, a Viking drinking horn raised on high, probably as he was thought to appear in the first bacchanalian banquet scene. In this scene, according to Johansen's costume list, twelve such knights and eight guests "changed from Skule's men" appeared, though there is no evidence to indicate that the costume depicted here was actually used. Nor does it seem possible to be entirely confident about the authorship of the sketch, in which the expressive irony of Svend Johansen and his fondness for period pastiche seem such prominent factors. A puzzle of this kind admits of no definitive solution at present, but it at least serves to emphasize the verificational difficulties that persis-

39. Costume design for one of Skule's knights
in *The Pretenders*.(Bibliothèque Nationale, Paris)

tently confront the student of this vexed and complicated theatrical venture.

Johannes Poulsen, too, appears to have taken a hand in determining the costumes. Whatever deference he paid in print to Craig's ideas about an "imaginative" style of costuming that would sweep aside all realistic or archaeological considerations, in practice he himself chose to appear as Bishop Nikolas in a replica of episcopal canonicals that might even have conjured up memories of his father in the same role fifty-five years before—though a more direct source of inspiration may well have been Max Reinhardt's vivid impersonation in 1904 of Ibsen's scheming cleric.[10]

Poulsen's promptbook also contains an extremely interesting costume sketch of his own (ill. 40) which depicts Margrete, Haakon's queen, and which once again—judging from a notation in the lower right-hand corner of the page—was derived from his study of the fifteenth-century paintings of Hans Memling. Poulsen's accompanying notes describe the Queen, who was played with great lyricism and tenderness by Else Skouboe, in a sumptuous and historically authentic costume that would consist of a cape of sky-blue silk, richly lined and trimmed with ermine, beneath which she was to wear a matching corsage (bodice) of white ermine with blue trim over a dress of damask-colored (that is, bluish-red) silk. A glimpse of violet petticoat completed the tasteful color scheme of Poulsen's design, which matches the general scheme of operative color values given on the flyleaf of the promptbook (though blue, it will be remembered, was subsequently deleted as a possibility). The finishing touch to Margrete's costume was a splendid coronet, identified by a notation on the sketch as "krone fra gamle spil" [crown from old drama]—a notation that becomes comprehensible only after one recalls that the Danish title of Poulsen's first great success, his spectacular, Reinhardt-inspired production of the Hofmannsthal adaptation of *Everyman*, was *Det gamle Spil om Enhver*, or *The Old Drama of Everyman*. Visual reminiscences from this popular production, which in 1914 had established Poulsen as one of this century's foremost Scandinavian directors, were to be found even yet in the borrowed *Everyman* costumes that were worn by some of the minor characters and crowd figures in *The Pretenders*.[11] Whether Poulsen's concept for Margrete's costume—which seems so much closer to the spirit of Reinhardt than to either Craig's ideas of symbolic simplification or Svend Johansen's boldly ironic manner—was actually used on the stage, we do not

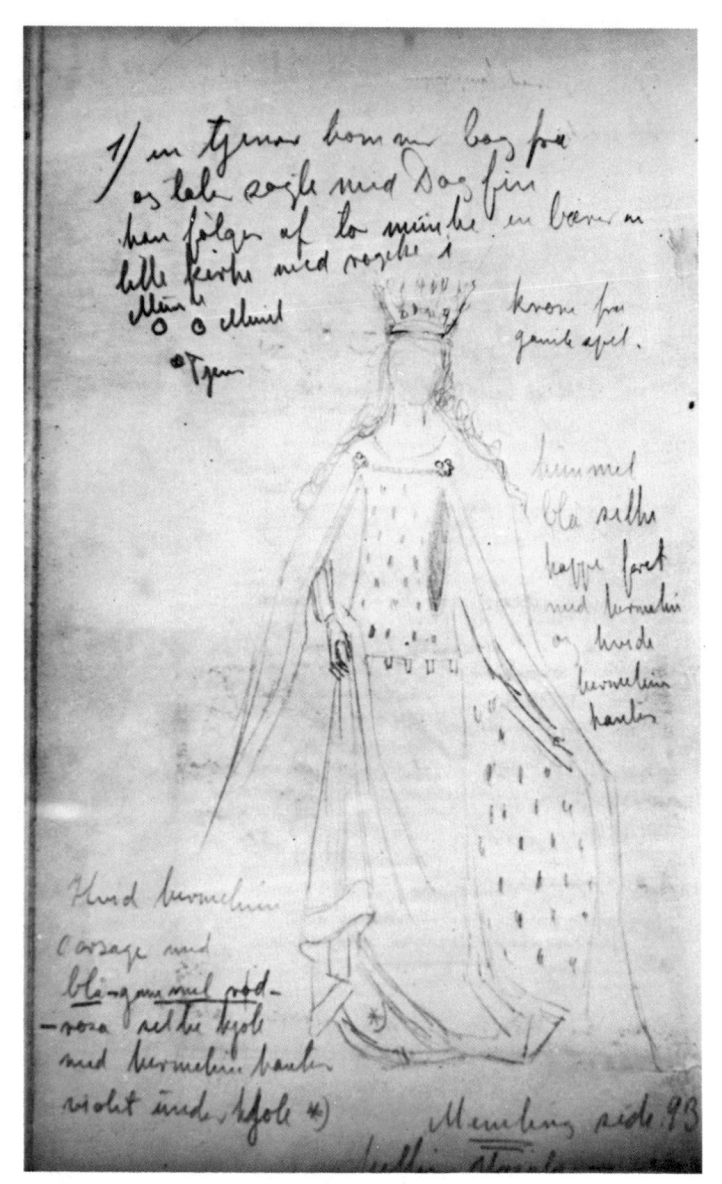

40. Sketch for Queen Margrete's costume
in *The Pretenders* included in Johannes Poulsen's
promptbook. (Royal Theatre Library)

know. Nevertheless, its existence provides yet another indication of the tendency toward an eclectic mixture of styles that characterizes this production.

The perceived absence of any single, unifying style of costuming in this performance may also help to explain Craig's relative neglect of this whole subject in his published accounts of *The Pretenders*. An "inseparableness of the dresses from their surroundings" which made them "essentially part of the design of each scene" had, from the very outset of Craig's career, been regarded as an outstanding feature of his production method—the quotation is taken from a review of his *Dido and Aeneas* (1900). In the Copenhagen experiment, however, this sense of integration was undercut by the implicit contradiction between his conception of abstract, deliberately dehistoricized scenes and a collection of picturesquely realistic costumes (for which he does not seem to have had sole responsibility) that gestured uncertainly toward a number of differing periods, places, and climates.

Craig appears to have departed from his earlier methods in a number of other ways as well. The overtly symbolic use of costumes (as, for example, the famous "cloak of golden porphyry" that covered the entire stage in the court scene in the Moscow *Hamlet*) was largely abandoned. In addition, unlike the simple, coarsely textured materials that predominated in so many of Craig's earlier productions, *The Pretenders* was all velvet and silk. "Elegance rather than roughness," reads a note in his interleaved copy of the text. "*The hair* neatly curled—combed—arranged.*" Only the cut leather and skins worn by a character like Dagfinn the Peasant offer at least some hint of Norse rusticity and at the same time recall the designer's earlier preoccupation with rough fabrics that could be transformed by lighting. In general, on the basis of the fragmentary and sometimes ambiguous evidence available, one is led to the conclusion that the costumes worn in Craig's final production succeeded in expressing the essential spirit and tone of Ibsen's saga figures only in occasional vivid glimpses, and not in any systematically conceptual manner.

# CHAPTER SEVEN

# DREAMS AND AFTERTHOUGHTS

When the final curtain fell at last, after nearly four hours, on the first jubilee performance of *The Pretenders*, Adam and Johannes Poulsen were recalled to the stage to accept the laurel crowns that are traditionally bestowed on such an occasion. Eventually the two actors were joined by a reluctant Edward Gordon Craig, who had spent most of the evening nervously pacing the streets in the vicinity of the theatre. Curtain calls were, until quite recently, never permitted for ordinary performances at the Royal Theatre. This, however, was an exceptional event, and the stage manager duly entered a terse record of it in the official Journal. After the three men had appeared together, "the fire curtain was (in accordance with management's orders) lowered immediately. The audience continued to clap for some time," this unemotional document informs us.

Just across Kongens Nytorv at the Hotel d'Angleterre, however, the celebration of the jubilee continued at a large formal banquet which received as much attention in the press as the production itself, and at which Johannes Poulsen and Craig each seemed suspiciously anxious that the "honor" of the achievement should befall the other. Moved by the spirit of the occasion, Craig abandoned the prepared text of a rather defensive speech that he had planned, but *Politiken* printed a translation of his manuscript alongside its review the next day. "You have seen only very little of *my* work in the performance this evening," he is pleased to insist at this juncture, "for in reality it has been my sole intention and my sole hope to be of some small use to

the two brothers, and it is to these two actors that I have offered my modest assistance. When I work for myself, I perhaps do so in a somewhat different manner, but here in Copenhagen I have served the actors." (The original of Craig's prepared text has apparently not survived, but a note scrawled hastily on a bit of cardboard captures the wry tone of his impromptu banquet address. "JP & AP Both are the sweetest natured people to assist—provided you do not assist them too much"!) The publicity surrounding the Craig-Poulsen collaboration rapidly subsided, however; long before the controversial and expensive production was withdrawn from the repertory, after its sixteenth and final performance on January 15, 1927, Craig had returned to his home just outside Genoa and to his "long game of patience."

A letter of thanks which he wrote to Johannes Poulsen from San Martino d'Albero radiates the most sympathetic qualities in his complex personality. "I am sorry that I squeaked now and again but *you* didn't and then don't forget you've been in the fire these last 15 years and I have not. So make allowances for me." Yet, here as in his undelivered version of the banquet speech, his exasperation at the inevitable practical realities of a normal rehearsal schedule colors his attitude toward the experience. "And though now and again I felt that my work was losing all its value through the *haste* with which it was served up, I do appreciate the difficulties you had to content with and realize that the only thing we *could* do was to rush it all through." (In his subsequent reply, Poulsen—with his usual blend of tact and good humor—proposed an American venture in which "you can make the stagings and I will use the *iron fist!*")[1]

In this as in so many other of Craig's statements about his last and—with the possible exception of the Moscow *Hamlet* which he produced with Stanislavski in 1912—most ambitious experiment in the practical theatre, one is struck by the evasively contradictory nature of his views. His repeated complaint that nothing had been prepared before he arrived in Copenhagen is, as we have seen, far from accurate, yet it is equally mistaken to suggest, as some have been misled into doing, that everything was finished and that he was engaged in the project in only a minor way. He must clearly be given full responsibility for the scenography, as a collation of his published designs with the theatre's floor plans helps to show, though he appears at times terribly anxious to obscure this fact. However, his insistence, in moments of greater self-confidence, that he not only

"ended up designing the entire play" but also, "with the assistance of Johannes," directed all the rehearsals stands in need of modification.

An even more basic ambivalence seems evident in his love-hate reaction to the theatrical traditions and customs which an institution like the Danish Royal Theatre or the Comédie Française virtually embodies—an ambivalence which permeates one of the impressionistic "illuminations" that make up an earlier manuscript first brought to light by Arnold Rood. "The old Theatre. Its smells its sounds Paint & Powder—a bustle of people in haste—real human beings concerned about pasteboard & tinsle—& themselves—appearing dressed up with their dear faces disguised. The bell rang—the curtain rose—the audience watched—once keenly, now strangely. The poor old Theatre had passed before they closed its doors."[2] "I have closed its doors—& its eyes," he continues in these reflections from 1913—but not before he adds a very significant comment about the "pretty artifice" of the traditional theatre. "I loved it better than all the others did."

Although Craig's complex and difficult emotional responses to a situation like the one in Copenhagen placed an understandable strain on his working relationship with Johannes Poulsen, the latter evidently remained eager to bring him back for another engagement—in spite of the fact that the internal crisis engendered by the troubled production of *The Pretenders* had precipitated Poulsen's temporary resignation from the Royal Theatre company at the close of the 1926–27 season. The sympathetic Danish actor-director seems to have done his best to help Craig in other ways as well—not least, it would seem from his letters, by putting him in contact with Per Lindberg, the pioneering Swedish director who, during the same season of 1926–27, presented a sensational program of open-stage productions at Stockholm's newly built Concert Hall.[3] How far actual negotiations between Craig and Lindberg may have progressed, we do not know with certainty—although a letter from Poulsen dated June 14, 1928, reveals plainly enough the (by now predictable) outcome. "Lindberg in Stockholm told me you have asked for several months for the rehearsal of *Twelfth Night*, but no theatre can give such a long time except in a few especially lucky cases. Do not be too brusque, but remember that goodness and gentleness take you far longer than if you strike the table and 'take the first train home.' " "Craig is an English gentleman," writes Lindberg in his own eminently balanced discussion of Craig's contributions, "he likes to play for high stakes, he may lose but he can never cheat."[4]

Standing in sharp contrast to the practical common sense which Poulsen tried, from time to time, to inject into their relationship are Craig's own private notations from this period—particularly his almost oneiric notes for a new theatre school, recorded with poignant determination in a small red-marbled notebook bearing the inscription "Summer Class 1927" (Collection Craig).

1st thing to do—to go to *Livorno*—see Teatro or Arena (if available) arrange—first for the place rent [space for price to be inserted] per year—failing *Livorno* go on to *Pisa*—try for one of the 2 theatres there—failing Pisa go on to *Lucca* & try there—Camogli [following cities added in pencil in the margin:] Perugia? Bologna? Napoli? Pompeii? Reggio-Emilia? Modena? Parma? Failing to find a theatre find an Arena or a large Palazzo with a vast extra hall—or church disused as in France.

Page after page of the little notebook is filled with schemes and "practical" arrangements for the school Craig envisioned (to be headed, it would seem, by the late Allardyce Nicoll, who might well have been surprised by the invitation). This dream, like so many others, came to nothing—but, as we have seen this long-established dreamer insist more than once, "a dream once dreamed properly *is* a reality inasmuch as it is worked out from beginning to end."

During these next few years, Craig met from time to time with Poulsen and his wife in Genoa, in London, and in Denmark, and otherwise maintained a faithful, if somewhat erratic, correspondence with them which paints a graphic and touching picture of his position during one of the most tragic periods of his career. "Will you hear about me? I work—I am terribly alone. I *ache* for my theatre," he writes early in 1928. "I *love* to work with you two—I dont say that ever to people. I like also to work unseen and unknown—then I work *well*—and if a special good Craigish bit of work appears and looks all right then I like to sign it—not otherwise. Then its a pleasure like a well *deserved* dinner after a long walk."[5] His frustrated contempt for a contemporary theatre that appeared to ignore him focusses, in these letters, on his archenemy Max Reinhardt, despite (or perhaps even because of) the fact that Poulsen was a professed admirer of Reinhardt's methods. "All this Reinhardt. 12 Theatres—Berlin—Mirakles, new wife, is getting a bit of a bore on a rather flat plane," he writes from Weimar in the fall of 1927, after an unsettling visit to Berlin.

"La mode"—REINHARDT—modern age—MACHINE—LONDON—JAZZ—Reinhardt—Mirakle—Russia—Meyerhold—Stanislavsky—Tairov.—Ma-

chine—Jazz—zzzzzz—zzzzzz—Berlin—Machine—Piscator Bühne—Paris—
Russland—new wife—Miracle. LA MODE—last mode—next mode—new
wife—aber is not this a little langweilisch?

So it is necessary, if one wishes to move on clearly, to stop and let the noise
die away.

Perhaps a certain E. G. C. has stopped too long—we shall see.[6]

Time and again Craig urged upon Poulsen the precarious idea that
the latter should give up acting for an entire year so that together they
might form "a company of clever beings—the best in Europe" in
order to "set out together to make more money and a bigger splash
than has yet been made by anyone." "Dont get old—get more dashing
J. P.—gamble for the biggest," this particular letter implores—re-
minding one inevitably of Lindberg's wry assessment of the imprac-
tical "English gentleman."

At this juncture, however, the otherwise imperturbable Poulsen,
endeavoring to earn his living as a free-lance artist following his
involuntary separation from the Royal Theatre, exploded. "Do not
walk about on the coast of Italy philosophizing like a Hamlet on the
stupidity of man and the follies of theatre-people, but come to London on the 1st of July when Ulla and I are there, and let us form our
schemes. It is not necessary to use a year for this, no, a few weeks or a
month will do. I already know exactly what we will make and I only
wait for discussing it with you." In a postscript characteristic of his
personality, Poulsen adds: "Reading this letter now on the machine I
find it hard—but *a friend* must have right to say the hard things and
*you* owe the English speaking people to do the great English theatre—
Everybody is waiting for you to do that."[7] Craig and Poulsen did in
fact meet frequently in London during that summer of 1928, and their
eager discussions seemed for a while to hold the promise of an
important new collaboration—until the death of the aged Ellen Terry
on July 21 drove any further thought of future plans from the mind of
her grief-stricken son.

Craig derived renewed hope from letters from the Poulsens
announcing the controversial appointment, early in 1930, of Adam
Poulsen to the post of managing director of the Royal Theatre in
Copenhagen. This providential event seemed momentarily to offer
him the one opportunity he so desperately sought—to stage another
production on his own terms, in a theatre and a context he could
respect. The undisguised disdain he had previously shown for the
commercially motivated commission from George Tyler (to whom

the helpful Johannes Poulsen had written on Craig's behalf) to provide the "designment" for the New York production of *Macbeth* is well
known. "He cribbed outrageously from his work in Copenhagen,
even using old drawings he had discarded two years earlier," declares
his son.[8]

Early in the summer of 1930, however, Johannes Poulsen arrived at
San Martino d'Albero with a proposal that was bound to elicit a very
different kind of response from Craig—an invitation, approved by the
Royal Theatre management, to collaborate with him on a new production of Shakespeare's *A Midsummer Night's Dream* in Copenhagen.
This fresh opportunity (not mentioned by Edward Craig or his other
biographers) at once filled Craig with a new sense of purpose that
suffuses a letter he wrote to Poulsen on June 27, 1930.

> Since you went I have taken up *A Midsummer Nights Dream* and *I could do
> that*—YES:
>> "*M. Nights Dream*"!!
>> "*The Beggars Opera*"!!
>> "*Macbeth*"!!
>> "*The Masque of Love*"!!
> All 4 I would do with delight. "*Julius Caesar*"!!! *What?*
>
> Yours E. G. C.

In a characteristic postscript he adds: "If I am to do some things I must
ask for *plenty of time*."[9]

A design concept for this new venture apparently took shape
quickly in Craig's mind, however, and his subsequent letters press
Poulsen for more news of the project. Writing from London in the
fall, where he had been invited by Charles B. Cochran to design and
perhaps also to direct an opening production for the new Phoenix
Theatre, his thoughts were still with the playhouse on Kongens
Nytorv. "I wish that I was made *something* to do with the ROYAL
THEATRE. A special friend adviser of it or something—so that I might
call to look at it twice a year and be of use to you all."[10] The
association with Cochran, like so many of Craig's collaborations in the
past, soon ended in smoke—the airy high-handedness of Craig's
attitude is painfully evident in John Gielgud's recollection of his first
encounter with his famous second cousin at this juncture.[11] At the
same time an even greater disappointment awaited him. The welcome chance to join Poulsen in producing Shakespeare at the Royal
Theatre—an undertaking that might well have had the kind of impact

on the Scandinavian theatre that Craig's somewhat inconsistent approach to Ibsen had lacked—was abruptly and irrevocably lost when Adam Poulsen, whose regime had already stirred up considerable internal dissent, fell ill at the beginning of 1931 and was peremptorily relieved of his post.

In fact, even before this contretemps, it must be said that Adam never shared his brother's confidence in Craig's abilities. Their first meeting in Berlin in 1906 had left the elder Poulsen with the impression of a fundamentally unoriginal "follower of those artists who, around the turn of the century, had formed a circle around that excellent periodical, *The Studio,*" and his experience with those "huge, box-like blocks which the actors were obliged to sit and move among" in *The Pretenders* did not lead him to change his mind. His thank-you note to Craig following the production had been all elegance and courtesy—"You came with sunshine and clearness and it is something we stand in need of *here,* where the fogs sometimes are lying close over country and people!"—but his true opinion animates the ironic description in his memoirs. "Henrik Ibsen has undoubtedly envisioned the settings for the play as a colorful accompaniment to the period flavor expressed in its dialogue and atmosphere—a fact which also emerges from his own stage directions. He did not intend the characters of the drama to make their entrances and exits between packing cases instead of through doors."[12]

One of Gordon Craig's last contacts with Johannes Poulsen, whose faith in Craig's methods never wavered but whose own brilliant career was cut short by his untimely death in 1938, is a long letter written by him from a small pension in Boulogne-sur-Mer, where he had gone to live with his young secretary after ruthlessly abandoning Elena Craig in Genoa. (One senses Poulsen's disgust with that act of disloyalty: he never acknowledged the letter from Boulogne-sur-Mer, and his last personal communication with Craig is in the form of an invitation to his fiftieth birthday party, pointedly addressed to "Mr. and Mrs. Edward Gordon Craig" and bearing the following note. "You know I was in Genoa again this summer, but you weren't there—unfortunately—How is your wife and Nelly and [the dog] Talma?") Craig's own letter, reflecting as it does his many disappointments, illustrates that familiar and abiding tension in his writing between sentimentality and redeeming self-irony, arrogance and generosity, bitterness and resignation.

I left England in a rage, not loud but deep—because of their dam stupid reception of me; and I think it would be a very strange happening should I ever again see England—except by accident. . . .

I go to Holland . . . then to Germany and Russia perhaps—I go to ask 3 or 4 cities if I may be allowed to *produce* one play, or even *design* one piece—or one scene.

I am a beggar without a home, and so I must take what I can get. . . .

Still, "BLESSED IS HE WHO EXPECTS NOTHING, FOR HE SHALL NEVER BE DISAPPOINTED" (at which words the organ plays off stage).[13]

A short postscript adds one more small but essential touch to the impression left by this unpredictable man of genius—the uneasy feeling that one never does quite know where he stands.

—but *after all*—what a silly play "The Pretenders" is—mais oui, alors!!!

APPENDIX

NOTES

BIBLIOGRAPHY

INDEX

# APPENDIX

## CRAIG'S REHEARSAL MEMORANDA

[The following document consists of memoranda compiled by Gordon Craig during the penultimate dress rehearsal for *The Pretenders*, held on November 12, 1926. Craig's rough handwritten notes and a fair, typed copy of them, presumably prepared by the Royal Theatre, are in the Collection Craig, Bibliothèque Nationale.]

### NOVEMBER 12

*Suggestions.* (notes made rapidly in the dark about the small errors to be put right.)
*Dagfinn:* the arms to be in a darker tone.

*Scene 1 (Church)*
No light to begin with. Bell to start play. Light to grow very slowly and not fast—last through the 1st song.
Opening of scene: *Skule* not in his right position, too far downstage. Must wear his circular red cloak as arranged.
Cut doors out, if they open so badly as they did.
Cut out the halo behind bishop, unless it can be carried well.
The scream is stupid—it should be a *slight* cry.
*Inga* not to look like the witches in Macbeth—she is a queen.
*Hakon:* head dress—the side pieces in blobs, to be bronzed like dark grey bronze.
As I see it all the costumes of Scene 1 wrong colours, because chosen without showing to any one and me.

With the actors the *groups* are not clear, they meddle together.

Should suggest that the *faces* have some light—at present the actors have none—only one well lighted, and he is a statist [supernumerary] in corner.

Yellow cloaks of Birchlegs to be cut.

Music to be at Hakon's and Skule's exit—or the exits seem (to me anyhow) flat.

### Scene 2 (Little Room)

Light comes up too suddenly—Why? In European Theatres one generally brings it up slowly.

In the long grey wall at back, the division where the steps come is too clear.

The song sung by woman spinning was to have been two songs, one a sad song and one a gay song.

In my opinion, *Margrete's wig* will not do, either in colour or shape.

Inside of roof of bigger house to be more flat and no creases.

There was no light on Margrete's face at window.

### Scene 3 (Baldachino)

The *Baldachino* to be kept straight.

*Dagfinn:* too pale the dress. The head dress far too big and unreal—the head itself too huge. A small head seems to me better.

*Skule* not to stand so long facing the audience, unless something to express.

*Vegard* not to cross as he does, when he goes out.

*Exit Margrete with Hakon* looked foolish—he went first and she ran after.

"A few new costumes have been specially made." I feel that this should be announced.

*Curtain*—to come slowly across—oil is useful.

*No light* at present on it.

The *music* to cover the wait, not to end and leave a pause.

*Too long a division between scene 3 and 4.*

### Scene 4 (Hakon's Banquet)

*Gold screen* still *glares.*

*Musicians* should be in red and darker *colours*, not in night gowns.

" to have sensible good wigs and not red things looking funny.

*3rd musician* to wait longer before he makes exit, otherwise strikes me as comic.

*Hakon's* Head good—*star on chest bad.*

The music at Hakon's exit squeaks and is late in the beginning.

Why does Hakon exit dragging Marguerite [*sic*]?

The *lights* at exit of Hakon to do something—all they do is to glare.

*Skule* in the scene with Bishop to ruffle up his *front* hair.

During *scene Bishop & Skule* the lights to change—and change again—to

green, purple and blue on screens at back, but remain warm colour on front.
The *stand for the banners* to be *cut*. Holes for other flags to be on the platform.
"Fruit & flowers" piece to be on the screen on right (Petersen).
Only *one* trumpet sounded during tournament.
*Birchlegs* come in too late behind Hakon—so best tell *Hakon* to come *last*.
*The Messenger* who speaks to Hakon to be in a proper neat quiet dress, not
looking like a shepherd or a wild man of Borneo.
Are the women in this scene to look like sticks?
Sigrid not to be pathetic in her appeal to Hakon.

*Scene Bishop's Death*
   The right corner of scene was perfectly lighted, fixed and written down 6
days ago.
   Now the effect has been lost—Why? Any good to restore it?
   *Inga* to enter gliding, not stumping along—to enter quickly not taking 3
minutes.
   *Dagfinn*—more dignity—too much Pantalone.
   Celebrated actor and actress bang the floor in quiet scene, as they exit. Inga
and Dagfinn both did so. Please look at their boots.
   *Storm music.* The music performed consisted of 3 pieces. We only heard
one???
   *Hakon's head dress:* too operatic in this scene.

*Bed scene [3. 2]*
   A good light was once arranged to show up Hakon. Some one has forgotten
it.
   *Skule* to exit at side—*not* through the stripes [that is, the ribbon backdrop].

*Skule's Banquet [4. 1]*
   White cloak to be removed from throne.
   Throne not to be twisted round so suddenly, but in 2 or 3 slight touches
brought round.
   [Craig's notes make no comment on act 4, scene 2, "A Street in Oslo." In
general, it will be noticed that his comments become much less detailed for
those scenes during which Johannes Poulsen was himself able to watch the
rehearsal from the front—that is, from act 3, scene 2, through act 5, scene 1.]

*Window-scene [5. 1]*
   The *light on the strips* should NOT be a *dark blue* light.
   *Ivar Bodde* and *Paul Flida not* to look comic (hair, heads).

*Scene Bishops's ghost*
   The snow far too white & distracts the eyes—dazzles them.

*Petersen* to paint with GREY and LESS LIGHT on the snow.

The pieces to have wood removed and *add soft pads* in place as weights.

There was *not sufficent light on Bishop's* face.

The laugh at end was *too short*, and should be three times as long & rise.

### Last Scene

May I again suggest *straight white lines* in sky, not curved ones.

*Skule* not to make noise with feet in coming in.

*Red light far too strong.*

When *soldiers* shut red gate there should be more noise of locking it and of chain.

The townsmen should not be so loud, should create a soft *hum* of low voices first—then *gradual* crescendo. And when at the red gate should *never* be quite silent.

# NOTES

CHAPTER I. CRAIG'S LAST PRODUCTION

1. William Butler Yeats, *The Letters of W. B. Yeats*, ed. Allan Wade (London: Rupert Hart-Davies, 1954), p. 398.
2. Quoted in Denis Bablet, *Edward Gordon Craig* (London: Heinemann, 1966), p. 88.
3. E. Corradini in *Vita d'arte* (March, 1908) 1, n. 3; quoted in Ferruccio Marotti, *Gordon Craig* (Bologna: Cappelli, 1961), p. 85.
4. Cf. Edward Gordon Craig, *On the Art of the Theatre*, 5th ed. (London: Heinemann, 1957), p. 22. This design, although much less frequently seen than the others mentioned previously, was exhibited at Henie-Onstads Kunstsenter, Høvikodden, Norway, in 1971, and was reproduced in the exhibition catalogue, entitled *Vår tids scenebilde* [Stage designs of our time].
5. One exception is a brief but highly untrustworthy article by Mogens Hyllested, "*The Pretenders:* Copenhagen 1926," *Theatre Research* 7 (1966): 117–22, which summarizes some of the Danish sources (mostly the newspaper reviews). Unfortunately, this critic has the tendency to misinterpret or even entirely overlook relevant sources in the Royal Theatre archives (as well as to ignore completely the Collection Craig in Paris), with the result that he is led to present as fact some extremely misleading conclusions.
6. An attempt to suggest, in condensed form, a means of approaching the production in this manner is found in Frederick J. Marker and Lise-Lone Marker, *The Scandinavian Theatre: A Short History* (Oxford: Basil Blackwell, 1975), pp. 228–32.
7. Cf. Ferruccio Marotti, "Problems of Documentation: Stage Management of Edward Gordon Craig," in *Regie in Dokumentation, Forschung*

*und Lehre* [Stage production in documentation, research and teaching], ed. Margret Dietrich (Salzburg: Otto Müller, 1974), pp. 43–46.

8. L. M. Newman, *Gordon Craig Archives: International Survey* (London: The Macklin Press, 1976), p. 11.

9. Edward Gordon Craig, *A Production* (London: Oxford University Press, 1930), p. 1. Further references to this work are given within the text.

10. The general point raised by Marotti concerning photographs of Craig performances is, however, worth noting. "Contray to what we used to think, the photographs are the least illuminating and the most difficult to interpret, in so far as in performances of this kind the presence of any particular actor is the least important"—that is, the camera's selective focus on a specific performer or grouping inevitably distorts the *totality* of impression to which a Craig production is dedicated. See Dietrich, *Regie in Dokumentation*, p. 44.

11. Craig's letters to Poulsen are published in a volume compiled by Poulsen's widow, Ulla Poulsen Skou, entitled *Genier er som tordenvejr: Gordon Craig på Det Kongelige Teater 1926* [Men of genius are like thunderbolts: Gordon Craig at the Royal Theatre, 1926] (Copenhagen, 1973). This collection contains thirty-six letters (some of them very brief notes), all but one of which stem from the period between 1925 and 1932. Regrettably (and inexplicably, in view of its official sponsorship by Selskabet for dansk Teaterhistorie), this volume fails to include the Poulsen half of the correspondence (found in the Bibliothèque Nationale) and even omits an important letter by Craig himself (his reply to Poulsen dated September 17, 1926), thereby weakening its scholarly usefulness considerably.

## CHAPTER 2. STAGE HISTORY

1. Specifically the third part of P. A. Munch's *Det norske Folks Historie* (1857), which treated the civil wars from the accession of King Sverre in 1177 to the fall of Duke Skule in 1240. Cf. Halvdan Koht in Francis Bull, Halvdan Koht, and Didrik Arup Seip, *Ibsens drama: Indledninger til Hundreårsutgaven* [Ibsen's drama: introductions to the centenary edition] (Oslo: Gyldendal Norsk Forlag, 1972], p. 19.

2. Cf. Marker and Marker, *The Scandinavian Theatre*, p. 130.

3. Johanne Luise Heiberg, *Et Liv gjenoplevet i Erindringen* [A life relived in memory], 3d ed., 2 vols. (Copenhagen: Gyldendal, 1913), 2: 346–47. Translations throughout this volume are by its authors.

4. Edvard Brandes, *Dansk Skuespilkunst* [The art of acting in Denmark] (Copenhagen: P. G. Philipsen, 1880), pp. 342–43.

5. Skou, *Genier er som tordenvejr*, p. 17.
6. In a letter to Ludvig Josephson dated June 14, 1876, quoted in Michael Meyer, *Ibsen: A Biography* (Hammondsworth, Middlesex: Penguin Books, 1974), p. 430.
7. Max Grube, *The Story of the Meininger*, trans. Ann Marie Koller (Coral Gables, Fla.: University of Miami Press, 1963), p. 81.
8. Cf. Per Bjurström, *Teaterdekoration i Sverige* [Stage design in Sweden] (Stockholm: Natur och Kultur, 1964), p. 66.
9. Georg Nordensvan, *Svensk teater och svenska skådespelare* [Swedish theatre and Swedish actors], 2 vols. (Stockholm: Bonniers, 1918), 2: 363.
10. Ibid., 436.
11. *Berliner Zeitung*, October 8, 1904, quoted in Heinz Kindermann, *Theatergeschichte Europas* (Salzburg: Otto Müller, 1968), 8: 311.
12. Henrik Ibsen, *The Oxford Ibsen*, ed. James Walter McFarlane (London: Oxford University Press, 1962), 2: 21.
13. The Yale production is commemorated by an acting version of the play, edited by Dwight Raymond Meigs and published by the Yale University Dramatic Association (New Haven, 1907). In his introduction to this interesting illustrated volume, the redoubtable William Lyon Phelps hails *The Pretenders* as "one of the Master's greatest works," adding that "the fact that Bernard Shaw omits this play entirely in his account of Ibsen's dramas is also a point in its favor" (p. xix)!
    In the Minneapolis production more than seventy years later, the approach to staging was determined in large measure by the particular demands of the Guthrie thrust stage. On a prodigiously deep platform that had been opened up at the back, designer David Lloyd Gropman deployed massive, movable set components, at once rough-hewn and intricately carved, that suggested to the reviewers of the production "the barbaric guts and the increasing refinement of this transitional period. Carved monoliths open into church doors." Costumes of rough, heavy homespun added to the critics' impression of "a dark-hued medieval ambience filled with deft touches of illumination." Above all else, perhaps, Craig in particular would have been baffled by the almost Charles Kean-like preoccupation with historicity that informs a lengthy program notice proclaiming the production's desire to "present you with a slice-of-life from centuries ago" and to "increase your enjoyment by making props and set-pieces seem more startlingly realistic. . . . We value authenticity at the Guthrie because we know it adds a special dimension to every play" (*The Guthrie Theater Program Magazine*, no. 1, 1978, p. 28).
14. *The Spectator* 110 (February 22, 1913): 316.
15. Quoted by Michael Meyer in his translation of *The Pretenders* (Lon-

don: Rupert Hart-Davies, 1964), p. 112. Meyer identifies the author of the review as H. C. Bailey, the detective novelist.

16. Quoted and discussed in Sybil Rosenfeld, *A Short History of Stage Design in Great Britain* (Oxford: Basil Blackwell, 1973), p. 139.

17. Program note for *Dido and Aeneas*, Hampstead Conservatory, May 17–19, 1900; quoted in Denis Bablet, "Edward Gordon Craig and Scenography," *Theatre Research* 11 (1971): 11.

18. Edward Gordon Craig, *Towards a New Theatre: Forty Designs for Stage Scenes with Critical Notes by the Inventor* (London and Toronto: J. M. Dent, 1913; reprinted New York: Benjamin Blom, 1969), p. 51.

19. "Gordon Craig om Teatret og Digterne" [Craig on theatre and playwrights], *Berlingske Aftenavis*, October 27, 1926. Craig's emphasis.

20. *The Mask* 12 *bis* [13] (January, 1927), 24n. Craig's emphasis. Craig's typed draft of the "interview" is among his papers in the Bibliothèque Nationale. On the various pseudonyms used by Craig and Lees, see Bablet, *Edward Gordon Craig*, pp. 114–15.

21. Like those used as early as 1902 by Craig for *Acis and Galatea*, in which "a white tent" consisted of long white ribbons—strips of upholsterer's webbing—suspended from the flies against a pale yellow background. "The floating strips formed a kind of linear ballet, to which the movements of costumes responded and contributed," comments Bablet in *Edward Gordon Craig* (p. 49).

22. *Aftenbladet*, November 15, 1926.

23. *København*, November 15, 1926, in an article entitled "Adam og Johannes Poulsens Jubilæumsforestilling: Henrik Ibsens historiske Skuespil *Kongsemnerne* i irsk Iscenesættelse" [Adam and Johannes Poulsen's Jubilee Performance: Henrik Ibsen's historical drama *The Pretenders* in Irish *mise en scène*].

24. *Ekstra-Bladet*, November 15, 1926.

25. Vilhelm Saxtorph, "Iscenesættelsen af *Kongsemnerne*" [The staging of *The Pretenders*], *Berlingske Tidende* (*kronik*), December 13, 1926.

CHAPTER 3. CRAIG COMES TO COPENHAGEN

1. Copy of the letter is in the Collection Craig, Département des Arts du Spectacle, Bibliothèque Nationale; cf. Skou, *Genier er som tordenvejr*, p. 127.

2. This and other letters from the Poulsens are in the Bibliothèque Nationale.

3. Instruktionsbog 1926 [director's script], stamped Dr. Vilh. Branners Samling 1081. Interleaved ms., 238 pp., with cuts, blocking, diagrams, instructions, occasional pencil drawings (Royal Theatre Library).

4. Cf. Skou, *Genier er som tordenvejr*, p. 26.
5. Det Kongelige Teaters Journal [The Royal Theatre journal], 1922–28 (ms., Royal Theatre Library).
6. Based on notations in a small red, marbled notebook, marked "Copenhagen 1926" on its cover (Bibliothèque Nationale).
7. "En verdensberømt Gæst paa Det Kgl. Teater—Besøg hos Shakespeare-Fornyeren Gordon Craig" [A world-famous visitor to the Royal Theatre—interview with Shakespeare reformer Gordon Craig], *Nationaltidende*, October 7, 1926. A comparable interview appeared in *Politiken* the same day.
8. *The Mask* 13 (January, 1927): 26.
9. Skou, *Genier er som tordenvejr*, p. 128.
10. Letter to Poulsen dated October 9, 1926, in Skou, *Genier er som tordenvejr*, p. 129.
11. Identified as no. 206 in *Gordon Craig et le renouvellement du théâtre* (Paris: Bibliothèque Nationale, 1962). Gösta M. Bergman takes up the important question of Craig's contribution to stage lighting in *Lighting in the Theatre* (Stockholm: Almqvist and Wiksell, 1977), pp. 330–39.

CHAPTER 4. REHEARSALS

1. Skou, *Genier er som tordenvejr*, p. 31.
2. Svend Johansen, *Et af Rafaels guddommelige forbilleder* [One of Raphael's divine models] (Copenhagen: Munksgaard, 1957), p. 76.
3. Edward Gordon Craig, *On the Art of the Theatre*, p. 99. Craig's emphasis.
4. Undated, unidentified newspaper clipping pasted into Craig's heavily annotated script for the play, an interleaved copy of R. Farquharson Sharp's edition of *"The Pretenders" and Two Other Plays* (London and Toronto, J. M. Dent; New York, E. P. Dutton, 1918), pp. xii, 316, listed as no. 204 in *Gordon Craig et le renouvellement du théâtre*.
5. Quoted in Skou, *Genier er som tordenvejr*, p. 110; the quotation here is retranslated from the Danish, Craig's orginal being unavailable.
6. Edward Gordon Craig, *On the Art of the Theatre*, pp. 75, 79.
7. Letter from London, dated October 1930 (Skou, *Genier er som tordenvejr*, p. 153). This rather pointed piece of advice was evidently offered "in exchange" for one of the candid bits of criticism which the actor sometimes sent Craig's way—"I shall remember carefully what you advised me to *not have too many ideas* and to work out *one* idea thoroughly. I am not foolish—and I can take advice thats good."
8. Edward Gordon Craig, *Henry Irving* (London and Toronto: J. M. Dent, 1930; reprinted New York: Benjamin Blom, 1969), pp. 146–47.

9. Craig's transcription of his notes, written on the Hotel d'Angleterre's music program for the 1926–27 season, is in the Bibliothèque Nationale. The letter to Poulsen, which differs in some details from the transcription, is printed in Skou, *Genier er som tordenvejr*, pp. 130–31.

10. Skou, *Genier er som tordenvejr*, pp. 37–38.

11. "Johannes Poulsen om *Kongsemnerne*'s Overraskelser" [Poulsen on *Pretender*'s surprises], *Dagens Nyheder*, November 14, 1926.

12. Notes on a flyleaf of Craig's interleaved script of the play (Bibliothèque Nationale, 204).

CHAPTER 5. THEORY IN PRACTICE

1. Lee Simonson is quick to seize the opportunity to belittle Craig on this count, as on so many others. "Here is elaborately recorded the fact that Craig at last understands that scenery must be moved swiftly if a production is to be successfully played. . . . In every art theatre in Europe and America speed of scene-shifting is so much a prime element in determining any design that it is taken as a matter of course. It would not occur to any one but Craig, who still thinks of himself as the centre of the theatrical universe, to record his most elementary mistakes for the enlightenment of his contemporaries." *The Stage is Set* (New York: Harcourt, Brace, 1932; rev. ed. New York: Theatre Arts Books, 1963), p. 333.

2. *Ekstra-Bladet*, November 15, 1926. All other newspaper references are to this date unless otherwise noted.

3. Saxtorph, "Iscenesættelsen af *Kongsemnerne*."

4. Edward Gordon Craig, *On the Art of the Theatre*, p. 157; cf. Bablet, *Edward Gordon Craig*, pp. 41–42.

5. Cf. Edward Gordon Craig, *On the Art of the Theatre*, p. 23.

6. A spacious stage by any standards: having a proscenium opening of forty-four feet and a working depth, with the cyclorama in place, of some seventy feet, Craig describes it as "equal in some measurements to Drury Lane and in others surprising it." (See *A Production*, pl. 1.)

In fact, however, the theatre's archives suggest that the opening crowd scene in the 1926 production might be viewed as relatively *modest* in proportion to the one managed by Fru Heiberg, on the much smaller stage of the old Royal Theatre, in 1871. In that early production, twenty-seven "men in armor," equipped with swords, shields, lances, axes, and longbows, were assigned to Haakon; twenty-one warriors, similarly armed, supported Skule; the "monks, nuns, and populace in Bergen" that crowded the churchyard

consisted of eight ballerinas, eight dancers, four ballet pupils, and
five female and two male members of the chorus; an apprentice and
four choirboys brought the total cast to eighty, excluding the eleven
principals in the scene. Regieprotokol [production protocol] 17.
januar [January] 1845 (ms. Royal Theatre Library), pp. 472-95.

7. Valdemar Vedel in *Dagens Nyheder* (the same review reappeared in
*Dagbladet*).

8. "Johannes Poulsen om *Kongsemnerne*'s Overraskelser."

9. Edward Gordon Craig, *A Production*, pl. 9.

10. Vilhelm Saxtorph in *Berlingske Tidende*, December 13, 1926.

11. Two-page ms. of lighting instructions, dated November 3 and signed
by Craig (Bibliothèque Nationale, 206).

12. Michael Neiiendam, ed., *Bogen om Johannes, skrevet af hans Venner*
[Commemorative volume about Johannes Poulsen, written and
published by his friends] (Copenhagen, 1945), p. 114.

13. Ibid., p. 115.

14. *Berlingske Tidende*, in a separate article on the scenery and the
audience that supplements Gulmann's review.

15. Critics who dismiss Ibsen's verse in this scene as "doggerel" seem to
overlook its ironic intent and its striking relationship in this respect
to J. L. Heiberg's satirical masterpiece, the "apocalyptic comedy" *En
Sjæl efter Døden* [A soul after death], 1840. In another sense as well,
as Michael Meyer remarks, "If this is doggerel, so is much of *Peer
Gynt*" (Meyer, *Ibsen*, p. 221).

16. Edward Gordon Craig, *On the Art of the Theatre*, p. 264.

17. Regieprotokol 17. januar 1845 and *Berlingske Tidende*, November 15,
1926.

18. For more information on Poulsen's staging of this ballet, see Svend
Kragh-Jacobsen and Torben Krogh, eds., *Den kongelige danske Ballet*
[The Royal Danish Ballet] (Copenhagen: Selskabet til Udgivelse af
Kulturskrifter, 1952), p. 368.

19. Skou, *Genier er som tordenvejr*, p. 129.

20. Edward Gordon Craig, *On the Art of the Theatre*, p. 74.

21. Preserved in the Bledlow Collection (Newman, *Gordon Craig Archives*,
p. 10).

22. Cf. Johanne Luise Heiberg, *Et Liv gjenoplevet*, 2: 348-49; for more
information in English about this production, see Marker and
Marker, *The Scandinavian Theatre*, pp. 128-30. Fru Heiberg's
promptbook is in the Royal Theatre Library, marked "Gl.
Instruktionsbog 1871" in later hand, handwritten ms., 390 pp., with
cuts, cues, occasional instructions.

23. Instruktionsbog 1899, marked Hr. Scene-Instruktør Lehmann, title
page signed Chr. Laurenberg, Interleaved ms., 219 pp. with cuts,
cues, blocking, instructions (Royal Theatre Library).

## CHAPTER 6. THE PROBLEM OF COSTUME STYLE

1. Cf. Frederick J. Marker, *Hans Christian Andersen and the Romantic Theatre* (Toronto and Buffalo: University of Toronto Press, 1971), pp. 144-45.
2. Cf. Robert Neiiendam, *Episoder og Personligheder fra Teatrets Verden* [Episodes and personalities from the world of the theatre] (Copenhagen: Nyt Nordisk Forlag, 1964), p. 73.
3. Edward Gordon Craig, *On the Art of the Theatre*, pp. 32-33.
4. Interview in *Dagens Nyheder*, November 14, 1926.
5. Terence Philip in *The Times*, January 9, 1912; see also *The Mask* 7 (May, 1915): 157-58.
6. Edward Craig, *Gordon Craig: The Story of His Life* (London: Gollancz, 1968), p. 289. Craig's emphasis.
7. Johansen, *Et af Rafaels guddommelige forbilleder*, p. 76.
8. Ibid., p. 77.
9. Otto Gelsted, *Svend Johansen* (Copenhagen, 1937), p. 9.
10. A good photograph of Reinhardt as Bishop Nikolas is reproduced in Kindermann, *Theatergeschichte Europas* 8, pl. 34, opposite p. 177.
11. Cf. Viben Bech, "Scenebilledet hos Ibsen—og dets realisation" [The stage picture in Ibsen—and its realization], in Jytte Wiingaard, ed., *Henrik Ibsen i scenisk belysning* [Ibsen in theatrical perspective] (Copenhagen: C. A. Reitzel, 1978), p. 125.

## CHAPTER 7. DREAMS AND AFTERTHOUGHTS

1. Craig's letter, dated December 3, 1926, is in Skou, *Genier er som tordenvejr*, p. 132; Poulsen's reply, dated March 20, 1927, is in the Bibliothèque Nationale.
2. Manuscript in the Department of Special Collections, University of California Library, Los Angeles. See Arnold Rood, " 'After the Practise the Theory': Gordon Craig and Movement," *Theatre Research* 11 (1971): 97.
3. Cf. Marker and Marker, *The Scandinavian Theatre*, pp. 226-28.
4. Per Lindberg, *Kring ridån: Studier i teaterns utveckling under femtio år* [Behind the curtain: studies in the development of the theatre during fifty years] (Stockholm: Bonniers, 1932), p. 76.
5. Letter dated January 23, 1928 (Skou, *Genier er som tordenvejr*, p. 139).
6. Letter dated November 2, 1927 (Skou, *Genier er som tordenvejr*, p. 137).
7. Poulsen's unpublished letter, dated June 14, 1928, is in the Bibliothèque Nationale; it replies to Craig's of May 16, 1928.
8. Edward Craig, *Gordon Craig*, p. 330.

9. Skou, *Genier er som tordenvejr*, p. 152.
10. Craig's letter is dated October, 1930, but his memorandum in a small notebook dated 1927 shows even more clearly what he had in mind. "For a Royal Theatre why should I not be appointed '*stage and acting inspector*' as in old and modern days this word inspector is something. With duties to visit once a year for a week or fortnight according to need & fee." (Bibliothèque Nationale)
11. Sir John Gielgud, *Distinguished Company* (Garden City, N.Y.: Doubleday, 1973), pp. 36–38.
12. Adam Poulsen, *En skuespillers erindringer: Aarene efter 1916* [An actor's memoirs: the year after 1916] (Copenhagen: Hirschsprung, 1962), pp. 153, 156; his letter to Craig, dated December 18, 1926, is in the Bibliothèque Nationale.
13. Both a draft and carbon copy of Craig's letter, dated May 31, 1931, and Poulsen's invitation of November 2, 1931, are in the Bibliothèque Nationale.

# BIBLIOGRAPHY

UNPUBLISHED SOURCES

*Collection Craig. Paris: Bibliothèque Nationale, Département des Arts du Spectacle, Poste 575.*

*The Pretenders.* Interleaved copy of R. Farquharson Sharp's translation, heavily annotated by Craig. Pp. xii, 316. Listed as no. 204 in *Gordon Craig et le renouvellement du théâtre.*
Typescript (7 pp.) and handwritten notes, marked "November 12."
Dress rehearsal notes, reproduced in the Appendix to this volume.
Lists and Remarks, including: Costume list, in Danish, signed Svend Johansen, dated 25 October 1926; "Kongs-emnerne 1899"—Danish Regieprotokol [production protocol] identifying props and costumes, with English translations added in pencil; fragmentary lists of props, music cues, and costume memoranda.
"Lighting," holograph (2 pp.) marked "Nov. 3rd as arranged for Mr. Poul Nielsen." Listed as no. 205 in *Gordon Craig et le renouvellement du théâtre.*
Costumes and Properties folder, containing fragmentary notes and sketches by Craig and Svend Johansen.
Folders (nine in all), containing notes and rough sketches by Craig for individual scenes in *The Pretenders.*
Sketchbook (folio), containing jottings and a self-caricature by Craig.
Marked proof sheets from Oxford University Press for *A Production.*
Small red, marbled copybook, in Craig's handwriting, marked "Copenhagen 1926."
Small red, marbled copybook, in Craig's handwriting, marked "Summer Classes 1927—what has to be got at once."

Correspondence with the Poulsen family, including drafts by Craig
and seven letters from Johannes Poulsen.
Diverse related correspondence, from the Royal Theatre management
and others.
Publicity material: "Mise-en-scène of the play *Kongsemnerne*, i.e., *The
Pretenders*" (typescript, 2 pp.); interview for *The Mask* (typescript,
9 pp.); transcript of newspaper controversy occasioned by
Parliamentary debate over Craig's invitation to Copenhagen
(typescript, 3 pp.).
Stage and costume designs, signed and dated (32), unmarked variants
(9), and large preliminary sketches (7) for *The Pretenders*.

*Royal Theatre Library, Copenhagen.*

Instruktionsbog 1926 [director's script], stamped Dr. Vilh. Branners
Samling 1081. Interleaved ms., 238 pp., with cuts, blocking,
diagrams, instructions, occasional pencil drawings.
Instruktionsbog 1899, marked Hr. Scene-Instruktør Lehmann, title
page signed Chr. Laurenberg. Interleaved ms., 219 pp., with cuts,
cues, blocking, instructions. Dated 29 May 1899.
"Gl. Instruktionsbog 1871" [old director's script], marked in later hand,
handwritten ms., 390 pp., with cues, cuts, occasional
interpretation.
Det Kongelige Teaters Journal [The Royal Theatre journal], 1922–28.
*Kongs-Emnerne.* 1st ed. Christiania, 1864. Marked Hr. Belysningsmester
[master electrician] Ludvigsen, title page signed Chr. Laurenberg.
Contains cuts, text changes, and occasional cues for the 1899
production.
Regieprotokol, 17. januar [January] 1845, pp. 472–75.
Signalbog [cue script] 1926, ms. containing music and light cues,
interleaved with *Kongsemnerne.* 5th ed. Copenhagen: Gyldendal,
1923.
Sufflørbog 1899 [prompt copy], handwritten ms., 393 pp., with cuts
and times.
Designs and preliminary sketches for costumes (15), 1871 production.
Designs by Svend Johansen for costumes (26), 1926 production.

PLAY TEXTS CONSULTED

Ibsen, Henrik. *Kongs-Emnerne.* 1st ed. Christiania: Johan Dahls Forlag,
1864.
————. *The Oxford Ibsen.* Ed. James Walter McFarlane. Vol. 2. London:
Oxford University Press, 1962.

———. *The Pretenders*. Ed. Dwight Raymond Meigs. New Haven: Yale University Dramatic Association, 1907.
———. *The Pretenders*. Trans. Michael Meyer. London: Rupert Hart-Davies, 1964.
———. *"The Pretenders" and Two Other Plays*. Trans. R. Farquharson Sharp. London and Toronto: J. M. Dent, 1918; New York: E. P. Dutton, 1918.

### BOOKS AND SCHOLARLY ARTICLES

Bablet, Denis. *Edward Gordon Craig*. London: Heinemann, 1966.
———. "Edward Gordon Craig and Scenography." *Theatre Research* 11 (1971): 7–22.
Bergman, Gösta M. *Lighting in the Theatre*. Stockholm: Almqvist and Wiksell, 1977.
———. *Den moderna teaterns genombrott 1890–1925* [Breakthrough of the modern theatre, 1890–1925]. Stockholm: Bonniers, 1966.
Bjurström, Per. *Teaterdekoration i Sverige* [Stage design in Sweden]. Stockholm: Natur och Kultur, 1964.
Brandes, Edward. *Dansk Skuespilkunst* [The art of acting in Denmark]. Copenhagen: P. G. Philipsen, 1880.
Bull, Francis, Halvdan Koht, and Didrik Arup Seip. *Ibsens drama: Indledninger til Hundreårsutgaven* [Ibsen's drama: introductions to the centenary edition]. Oslo: Gyldendal Norsk Forlag, 1972.
Craig, Edward. *Gordon Craig: The Story of his Life*. London: Gollancz, 1968.
Craig, Edward Gordon. *Ellen Terry and her Secret Self*. London: Sampson Low, Marston and Co., 1931.
———. *Henry Irving*. London and Toronto: J. M. Dent, 1930. Reprinted New York: Benjamin Blom, 1969.
———. *Index to the Story of My Days*. London: Hulton Press, 1957.
———. *On the Art of the Theatre*. 5th ed. London: Heinemann, 1957.
———. *A Production, Being Thirty-two Collotype Plates of Designs prepared or realized for "The Pretenders" of Henrik Ibsen and produced at the Royal Theatre, Copenhagen, 1926*. London: Oxford University Press, 1930.
———. *Scene*. London: Oxford University Press, 1923.
———. *The Theatre Advancing*. London: Constable, 1921.
———. *Towards a New Theatre: Forty Designs for Stage Scenes with Critical Notes by the Inventor*. London and Toronto: J. M. Dent, 1913. Reprinted New York: Benjamin Blom, 1969.
Craig, Edward Gordon, ed. *The Mask* 1–6 (1908–15); 8 (1918–19); 9 (1923); 10–15 (1924–29).
Dietrich, Margret, ed. *Regie in Dokumentation, Forschung und Lehre* [Stage production in documentation, research and teaching]. Salzburg: Otto Müller, 1974.

Gelsted, Otto. *Svend Johansen*. Copenhagen, 1937.

Gielgud, Sir John. *Distinguished Company*. Garden City, N.Y.: Doubleday, 1973.

*Gordon Craig et le renouvellement du théâtre* [catalogue]. Paris: Bibliothèque Nationale, 1962.

Grube, Max. *The Story of the Meininger*. Trans. Ann Marie Koller. Coral Gables, Fla.: University of Miami Press, 1963.

Heiberg, Johanne Luise. *Et Liv gjenoplevet i Erindringen* [A life relived in memory]. 3d ed. 2 vols. Copenhagen: Gyldendal, 1913.

Hyllested, Mogens. "The Pretenders: Copenhagen 1926." *Theatre Research* 7 (1966): 117–22.

Johansen, Svend. *Et af Rafaels guddommelige forbilleder* [One of Raphael's divine models]. Copenhagen: Munksgaard, 1957.

Kindermann, Heinz. *Theatergeschichte Europas*. Vols. 8, 9. Salzburg: Otto Müller, 1968, 1970.

Kragh-Jacobsen, Svend, and Torben Krogh, eds. *Den kongelige danske Ballet* [The Royal Danish Ballet]. Copenhagen: Selskabet til Udgivelse af Kulturskrifter, 1952.

Leeper, Janet E. *Edward Gordon Craig: Designs for the Theatre*. Hammondsworth, Middlesex: Penguin Books, 1948.

Lindberg, Per. *Kring ridån: Studier i teaterns utveckling under femtio år* [Behind the curtain: studies in the development of the theatre during fifty years]. Stockholm: Bonniers, 1932.

Loeffler, Michael P. *Gordon Craigs frühe Versuche zur Überwindung des Bühnenrealismus* [The early efforts of Gordon Craig to overcome stage realism]. *Schweizer Theaterjahrbuch* 25. Issued by the Schweizerischen Gesellschaft für Theaterkultur, 1969.

Marker, Frederick J. *Hans Christian Andersen and the Romantic Theatre*. Toronto and Buffalo: University of Toronto Press, 1971.

Marker, Frederick J., and Lise-Lone Marker. *The Scandinavian Theatre: A Short History*. Oxford: Basil Blackwell, 1975.

Marotti, Ferruccio. *Edward Gordon Craig*. Bologna: Cappelli, 1961.

Meyer, Michael. *Ibsen: A Biography*. Hammondsworth, Middlesex: Penguin Books, 1974.

Nash, George. *Edward Gordon Craig, 1872–1966* [catalogue]. London: Victoria and Albert Museum, 1967.

Nathansen, Henri. *Johannes Poulsen*. Copenhagen: Gyldendal, 1946.

Neiiendam, Michael, ed. *Bogen om Johannes, skrevet af hans Venner* [Commemorative volume about Johannes Poulsen, written and published by his friends]. Copenhagen, 1945.

Neiiendam, Robert. *Episoder og Personligheder fra Teatrets Verden* [Episodes and personalities from the world of the theatre]. Copenhagen: Nyt Nordisk Forlag, 1964.

Newman, L. M. *Gordon Craig Archives: International Survey*. London: The Macklin Press, 1976.

Nicoll, Allardyce. *English Drama, 1900–1930.* Cambridge: Cambridge University Press, 1973.

Nordensvan, Georg. *Svensk teater och svenska skådespelare* [Swedish theatre and Swedish actors]. 2 vols. Stockholm: Bonniers, 1918.

Poulsen, Adam. *En skuespillers erindringer: Aarene efter 1916* [An actor's memoirs: the years after 1916]. Copenhagen: Hirschsprung, 1962.

Rood, Arnold. " 'After the Practise the Theory': Gordon Craig and Movement," *Theatre Research* 11 (1971): 81–101.

———. *Edward Gordon Craig, Artist of the Theatre, 1872–1966* [catalogue]. Intro. by Donald Oenslager. New York: New York Public Library, 1967.

Rose, Enid. *Gordon Craig and the Theatre: A Record and an Interpretation.* London: Sampson Low, Marston and Co., 1931.

Rosenfeld, Sybil. *A Short History of Stage Design in Great Britain.* Oxford: Basil Blackwell, 1973.

Senelick, Laurence. "The Craig-Stanislavsky *Hamlet* at the Moscow Arts Theatre," *Theatre Quarterly* 6, no. 22 (1976): 56–122.

Simonson, Lee. *The Stage is Set.* New York: Harcourt, Brace, 1932. Rev. ed. New York: Theatre Arts Books, 1963.

Skou, Ulla Poulsen. *Genier er som tordenvejr: Gordon Craig på Det Kongelige Teater 1926* [Men of genius are like thunderbolts: Gordon Craig at the Royal Theatre, 1926]. Copenhagen: Selskabet for dansk Teaterhistorie, 1973.

*Vår tids scenbilde* [Stage designs of our time: catalogue]. Høvikodden, Norway: Henie-Onstads Kunstsenter, 1971.

Wiingaard, Jytte, ed. *Henrik Ibsen i scenisk belysning* [Ibsen in theatrical perspective]. Copenhagen: C. A. Reitzel, 1978.

Yeats, William Butler. *The Letters of W. B. Yeats.* Ed. Allan Wade. London: Rupert Hart-Davies, 1954.

## NEWSPAPERS

*Aftenbladet* (Copenhagen)
*Berliner Zeitung* (Berlin)
*Berlingske Aftenavis* (Copenhagen)
*Berlingske Tidende* (Copenhagen)
*B.T.* (Copenhagen)
*Dagens Nyheder* (Copenhagen)
*Ekstra-Bladet* (Copenhagen)
*København* (Copenhagen)
*Nationaltidende* (Copenhagen)
*Politiken* (Copenhagen)
*The Spectator* (London)
*The Times* (London)

# INDEX